W9-BUI-093

COMMUNITY COLLEGES, THE FUTURE, and SPOD*

*Staff, Program, and Organizational Development

Richard J. Brass, Editor

Future Trends Commission
National Council for Staff, Program, and Organizational Development
    an affiliate council of the
American Association of Community and Junior Colleges

NEW FORUMS PRESS, INC.
Stillwater, Oklahoma 74076

Library of Congress Catalog Card Number 84-61248

ISBN 0-913507-01-6

This book is available at a special discount when ordered in bulk quantities. For information, contact New Forums Press, Inc., P.O. Box 876, Stillwater, OK 74076.

Printed in the United States of America.

CONTENTS

". . . the structural make-up of the institution must be molded
to fit the direction of the future." Take four questions seriously.

"The integration of human development elements into the mainstream of the instructional process is an absolute necessity if we
hope to preserve what has been described as our greatest natural
resource, human productivity."

Hawaii's staff development system grew out of the determination
of the staff at all levels to improve the quality of their own performance. Can Hawaii's experience serve as a model for the rest
of us?

High technology telecommunication systems deliver staff development programming for the whole person, the college staff as well
as for staff of other organizations in the community.

SPOD professionals and other educators need to acquire the
mindset and skills with which to address the future. As change
agents, they need to construct communication plans/advocacy
strategies to impact and shape the future.

Courtney D. Peterson

"A genuine SPODer must be a futurist, with an ability to function in a world of constant flux and change. The challenges and opportunities for SPODers working in such a period of transition are limitless . . . only by accepting uncertainty as a constant companion will individuals and institutions remain adaptable enough to survive the rites of passage into the 21st century."

Roland Terrell

In order for SPOD to survive, much less to assertively and effectively accomplish its agenda and purpose within the college, it must become "institutionalized." We need to implement a strategic plan to accomplish this. "The future is literally in our hands . . ."

Editor's Notes

A few comments regarding SPOD, NCSPOD, and the origins of this book are in order.

WHAT IS SPOD?

Is it a new high performance miniature computer used by college business managers and comptrollers? Is it one of the spate of emergent personal development techniques filling up the front shelves of the nation's book stores?

No, SPOD is not a computer used by business managers. It does, however, encompass an array of theories and practical, down-to-earth activities and overall functions managed and sometimes lead by a college official charged with the responsibility of protecting and developing an institution's investment in its employees, its staff. The college's manager of human resources does many of the same functions with and for the college's personnel that a business manager does with and for the organization's money, funding sources, and capital investments.

No, SPOD is not an emergency personal development technique sold at book stores. It, however, is a function

1

which utilizes many activities and strategies through which organizational structures, policies and procedures are further developed and improved. It also is a function through which the college's staff—all staff—keep updated, and learn how to do their jobs with ever greater quality, effectiveness, and productivity. It supports, encourages, and facilitates the on-going personal and professional development of the college's greatest resource—its people—so they can serve students, society, and the emergent global community better.

SPOD is not new. As an acronym it stands for staff, program, and organizational development. SPOD is an umbrella term which refers to various functions and activities that are sometimes referred to as staff, management, support staff, program, curriculum, career, instructional, faculty, and/or organizational development. Generically, it is often referred to as human resource development or human resource management. SPOD is a crucial function for any college which desires to survive, to transverse the future effectively, and to remain vital, vibrant, and responsive to its expanding, changing community.

THE NATIONAL COUNCIL

The National Council for Staff, Program, and Organizational Development (NCSPOD) is the professional association for community and junior college SPOD practitioners in the United States and Canada. From its beginnings in the fall of 1977, NCSPOD has grown to become the single largest affiliate council of the American Association of Community and Junior Colleges. The purposes of NCSPOD are:

A. Fostering staff, program and organizational development activities in public and private two-year community, junior and technical colleges.

B. Fostering innovative and effective approaches to staff, program and organizational development.

C. Fostering means for self-development of persons interested in staff, program and organizational development.

D. Maintaining communication among offices and organizations concerned with staff, program and organizational development.

E. Fostering research and evaluation in the field of staff, program and organizational development.

THE FUTURE TRENDS COMMISSION

NCSPOD's Future Trends Commission is to alert the Council and its members to new trends in two-year post-secondary education and SPOD. It does this in a variety of ways—through presentations at national conferences, through regular articles in NCSPOD's nationally distributed newsletter, *Network*, through dissemination of pertinent literature and bibliographies on the future, and through generation of special concept papers deemed of special import to the profession. The 1982-83 Commission membership numbers 33 SPOD professionals located throughout most of North America.

THIS BOOK

Meeting in session at the NCSPOD national conference in Louisville, the Commission decided to focus its primary attention on three issues of paramount importance: educators as futurists and advocates, the implications of electronic technology for community colleges and SPOD, and the institutionalization of SPOD. The Commission decided to divide itself into three task forces for the purpose of writing a concept paper on these areas under the leadership of a principal writer for each. Each task force was to generate a brief bibliography of other references on its topic as well as specific recommendations for four groups. These are SPOD practitioners, local colleges, state associations, and the NCSPOD Executive Committee.

The relevance of these issues can be more easily acknowledged if they are viewed within the context of the changing community college scene of north and central North America. Because of this, and wanting to evoke other voices and views on the future, other American and Canadian writers were approached for manuscripts. A book format was judged to be

the best medium through which to share these ideas, analyses, predictions, and aspirations with SPOD practitioners
and two-year college leaders in this hemisphere, *Community
Colleges, the Future, and SPOD* was born.

THE TEAM

As is true of most significant projects, this book is the
result of the close teamwork of a number of people. First of
all, the members of the Commission came up with the idea
and actively supported it through contributing ideas and
resources of all types. The principal writers heading up each
task force, Pat Brams, Courtney Peterson, and Roland
Terrell, dedicated a year to researching, writing, and refining
their chapters. The NCSPOD Executive Committee placed
their confidence in the Commission's work and provided it
with great encouragement and support. The fourteen writers
of the book's first section demonstrated strong commitment
and dedication, writing high quality chapters within severe
time limitations. The Publications Commission, headed by
NCSPOD Vice-President for Publications Ed Haring and
assisted by Ed's staff at Elgin Community College (Illinois),
accomplished the ultimate magic tranforming a collection of
manuscripts into a fine, finished publication.

THE FIRST STEP

We have all of the people above to thank for bringing to
us the first major work on community colleges, the future
and SPOD. It is a fine first step. Much remains to be done . . .
reflecting, analyzing, probing, advocating, identifying issues,
sharing ideas, planning, taking individual and cooperative
action, assessing progress and replanning and revising. This
first effort will spur us on our way.

Iowa City Iowa   *Richard J. Brass*
June, 1984   *Editor*

ABOUT THE AUTHOR

RICHARD J. BRASS is a charter member of NCSPOD, chairperson of Future Trends Commission, and 1981 recipient of that organization's Individual Merit Award "for outstanding contributions to staff development." He is President of Brass, Richie and Betts, Inc. of Iowa City, Iowa and Oak Park, Illinois, a consulting firm specializing in serving community colleges. In the past, Brass was a community college instructor and administrator. Later becoming the Associate Director of the University of Iowa's Office of Community College Affairs, he worked with colleges in many areas of the country in addition to Iowa. He is a co-founder and past president of the Iowa Council for Staff, Program, and Organizational Development, Vice President of the Eastern Iowa Chapter of the American Society for Training and Development, and a member of the World Future Society.

Introduction

Richard J. Brass

AN ERA OF QUESTIONS

"We are living in the time of the parenthesis, the time between eras. The time of parenthesis is a time of change and questioning," states futurist John Naisbitt in his new book, *Megatrends*. In *The Turning Point*, author and physicist Fritjof Capra maintains that we are all involved in a world-wide transformation of values and perspective. "The major problems of our time are all different facets of one and the same crisis, which is essentially a crisis of perception," says Capra. "[The crisis] derives from the fact that we are trying to apply the concepts of an outdated world view—the mechanistic world view of Cortesian-Newtonian science—to a reality that can no longer be understood in terms of these concepts." Our reductionist approach to systemic problems has brought us to an impasse.

There certainly is an abundance of questioning going on . . . in finance, politics, world order, relationships, management procedures, and much more. Many organizations and professions are reflecting on questions of existence and purpose. In the scramble for answers, or at least organizing viewpoint, many areas of thinking, analysis and action are being probed. Some of these include long-range planning, futurism, organizational development, new management philosophies and procedures, different methods of relating, and the relatively new field of issues/policy management.

QUESTIONS IN EDUCATION

This questioning has not left the field of education untouched. At least four major reports on education in the United States have been issued recently, including the report of the President's Commission entitled *A Nation At Risk*. Leaders in two-year postsecondary educational institutions are questioning themselves regarding these reports and a blizzard of other pressures and forces of change. Many of the questions dig deep. They often deal with, "What should we be doing and how should we do it?"

As professional change agents and human resource managers for community, technical, and junior colleges, many SPOD professionals also find themselves caught in a confusing web of reflection, reevaluation and questioning. What should we be doing to best help our institutions be effective and responsive in the context of a new reality? What's the best way to do it? How can we decide these questions without assisting our institution to set its future course, its mission, values, and objectives? How can we help to create a shared vision of the future of the college by all our constituents?

THIS BOOK

This book is intended to explore this malaise along with its limitless opportunities. This volume seeks to share a national (United States) discussion regarding community colleges, the future, and SPOD. It seeks to deal with such questions as what's happening, who are we, where should we be going, what should we be doing and how/when should we do it? We are not hapless victims of a capricious future. We can construct our own view of a preferred future. We can analyze the trends around us in order to predict a probable future. We can put the two together and, in an active way, do much to shape the future in specific directions. What future do we want to/will we build?

THE WRITERS

Within these covers, seventeen writers share their perceptions, their analyses, their ideas, and their initial attempts at forging some directions and advocating a few solutions. They come from nine different states representing every region of the country—north, south, east and west. These men and women also represent a wide array of backgrounds. Some are community college administrators—presidents, vice presidents, vice provosts, deans, and managers. Some are local or state directors of staff and/or curriculum development. Two are formally trained futurists. One is a director of programming and two are heads of state agencies for community colleges. Several are members of NCSPOD and two are either former or present NCSPOD elected officers. One is a university professor of community college education, directs an office providing SPOD services to community colleges, and is the former president of two colleges. All are deeply committed to the community college and understand the important function SPOD has.

SECTION ONE — COMMUNITY COLLEGE CHALLENGES: VARIOUS PERSPECTIVES

In this section, fourteen writers share their perspectives on the challenges confronting our colleges. They either discuss the overall title of the book or a sub-set of issues included therein.

Lynn Willett gets our "gray-matter" activated by sharing twenty-four questions about the future which we need to address. The next three chapters (Anderson, Pickett, and Norris) address over-arching philosophical issues—questions about identity and purpose. General suggestions for community colleges and SPOD on both the state and local levels are pointed up in the next four chapters (Haring and Willett, Evans, Pierce and Bragg, and Garrison). The final four chapters of this section (Shepard, Ott, Tsunoda and Veregge, and Stewart) delve into specially targeted areas of concern in some depth. After finishing this section, you may find some of Willett's initial questions easier to address.

SECTION TWO — ADVOCACY, PREDICTIONS, AND APPLICATIONS: FUTURE TRENDS COMMISSION FOCI

Section One offers a wealth of analysis and abundant ideas for action. It also provides a national-climate setting within which to view the three Commission task force chapters of Section Two.

Each chapter of Section Two seeks to speak to the general situation of community colleges across the nation. Each offers a list of references for extended background reading. Each suggests a battery of specific recommendations to four groups. Those groups are SPOD professionals/practitioners, local colleges, state associations, and the NCSPOD Executive Committee.

LAUNCHING OUT

The Commission hopes this book gives us all some good, worthwhile ideas to implement. It also hopes these chapters cause us to formulate the many questions which still need to be asked.

We have an exciting future ahead of us. It's ours to build.

SECTION ONE
Community College
Challenges:
Various Perspectives

ABOUT THE AUTHOR

LYNN H. WILLETT is the Vice President
for Institutional and Community Development at Elgin Community College, Elgin,
Illinois and an adjunct instructor for Southern Illinois University. Currently an Associate Editor for *Community/Junior College
Quarterly for Research and Practice*, Willett
has published articles in at least seven other
academic journals. This former Dean of
Community Services has a Ph.D. degree in
Higher Education.

1

Twenty-four Questions About the Future

Lynn H. Willett

"What wine and cheese would be best for our trip into the future?" asked a futurist at the 1983 World Future Society Education Section Conference held in Dallas, Texas. This question was one of hundreds of questions and observations exchanged by futurists.

The hundreds of conference presentors and participants generated an enthusiastic exchange of strategies, hopes, and scenarios about the expanding educational future of the world. Gleaned from the convention presentations are a few questions which caught the writer's attention. Can you provide an answer?

1. Part of futurist methodology utilizes a strategy called developing your preferred future scenarios. What would be three things you would prefer to have happen in your career at the end of next year?

2. Since we all have what psychologists call an "extended self interest" in any investment of our energy, how can our human resource development efforts capitalize on this hidden motive?

3. Most of our teaching and learning efforts work toward convergent thinking, but, the important question is how can we begin to develop in ourselves skills and tolerance for divergent thinking?

4. Are minimum cutoff teaching competency scores for teachers going to improve educational quality?

5. How many can you name of the 190 new jobs projected for the year 2,000 by Cetron and O'Toole in *Encounters with the Future?*

6. How can I utilize micro-computers to improve my professional effectiveness?

7. How can we integrate our knowledge about life transitions into our teaching and learning approaches to students?

8. Some career choice counselors are achieving success with clients utilizing life-space graphing. First, chart out all of the key activities you are currently doing. Next, imagine that you are now living in the year 2,000. Now, what would you have left?

9. How can we articulate the importance of developing self-esteem for ourselves through volunteerism in unknown ventures?

10. How can we build effective learning network exchanges between our older and younger students?

11. What are five E.T.D.s (events, trends and developments) which will be affecting how you will work next year? These E.T.D.s are essential input into your strategy for answering question number 1.

12. The future forecaster, Marvin Cetron, emphasized that our task as leaders is to utilize consultative management strategies, not participative management involvement. Can you offer consultative advice to a colleague without requiring a long-term participative involvement?

13. The community is the place where learning best occurs. How can you utilize your local community as a resource in teaching or management?

14. Learning can be greatly facilitated in one-to-one mentoring relationships. What are some effective ways that you can identify and link mentors from the community with students and clients?

15. What does growing your own tomatoes and owning your own microcomputer have to do with one another?

16. Futurists say we are in a paradigm shift from the industrial to the technological information age but each new age generates its countercurrents. What are the human "high touch" educational and organizational responses to technology which we should anticipate in 1990?

17. How can we begin to learn how to learn?

18. What questions did I ask today for which I did not already know the answer?

19. What will I do with the free time that the microcomputer will provide for me and my associates?

20. Who in my organization and community is a futurist?

21. Barbara Marx Hubbard says there operates a recurrent designing process in nature leading to higher systems of greater order and sophistication. How can we participate in this process as co-creators?

22. Futurists predict that organizations will become flatter, less heirarchial. What does this mean to us as organizational developers and managers?

23. Robert Theobald says most of us professionals do not have the *minimum* skills to initiate cooperative projects. What are the organizational incentives which will encourage us to acquire cooperative skill building competencies?

24. What if we begin to live as long as trees?

The answer sheet for these questions does not exist. Each of us will be faced with finding our own answers to these and many other questions as we plunge into the Twenty-First Century. Perhaps our best hope of developing a coping strategy comes from how we answer question number

1. This question implies that we have input and can strategize to shape the future on our terms.

Now, back to that first question about the wine and cheese . . . well, it depends on what scenario you developed for yourself and where and with whom you plan to spend your future!

ABOUT THE AUTHOR

DUANE D. ANDERSON is an Associate Professor of Higher Education and Director of the Office of Community College Affairs at the University of Iowa. He holds a Ph.D. degree in Community College Administration and is the former president of two community colleges. Anderson is a consultant of Colleges and Secondary Schools and Chair of the Iowa Regents Committee on Educational Relations. This founding chair of the Iowa Professional Teaching Practices Commission, is also past president of the Iowa Higher Education Association and a member of the AACJC Governmental Affairs Commission and NCSPOD.

2
Toward Excellence
From a SPOD Perspective

Duane D. Anderson

Whether the Human Resource Manager is identified as a staff developer or is occupying another role that requires him or her to assume that responsibility as part of a larger job description, the change that is occurring in the community college mission will require a complete reorientation to that task.

The current emphasis on "excellence" may in fact signal the most revolutionary change in direction, and need for the most extensive staff, program, and organizational development effort in the past thirty years of community college development. Perhaps only twice before in the institution's eighty-year-old history have conditions called for change not only in amount but more importantly in "type" as exists today.

Herbert S. Kindler in his article "Two Planning Strategies: Incremental Change and Transformational Change" discusses the conditions under which incremental change is appropriate. Among these conditions he cites the following: 1. the assumptions of the current system are acceptable to stake holders; 2. a back log of incremental change possibilities is available; and 3. current rates of improvement are

19

economical. We have found in our past history that these
conditions do exist for relatively long periods of time within
the community college even though there are minor vari-
ations which on the surface would seem to make incremental
change an inappropriate strategy. It is under these conditions
that many staff development people have worked for most
of their professional lives and that incremental norm serves as
a model for nearly all of the current staff development programs and staff developer perceptions—mind set, if you will.

The second type of change called for by Kindler, is
termed transformational change. This type of change strategy
taken from a broad historical perspective probably occurred
first in 1917 when the existing two-year college mission
underwent a wrenching change epitomized but certainly not
entirely caused by the passage of the Congressional Smith-
Hughes Act. The rather stable "development" of the two-
year college prior to that time followed an almost universal
acceptance of the college serving as a preparatory institution;
enrolling high school graduates destined to transfer to a four-
year college; staffed by high school teachers with a basic
orientation to that type of student and that mission; controlled and financed by public school methods familiar to
parents, boards and society in general. An infusion on a
massive scale of the concepts, values, and procedures of
vocational educators, called for—but perhaps did not deliver—
a major developmental effort of the "transformational"
type.

The *standards* embraced by the college transfer oriented
institution and the faculty who staffed it were suddenly
being challenged by a new, strange, and disturbing set of standards. With our perfect 20/20 hindsight, we can now see that
rather than assimilating those standards and that value system
into the institutional philosophy, an uneasy truce was
worked out that allowed the two-year college system to expand rapidly, sometimes as a single institution, but often
developing into two different institutions each embracing
its own standards. Obviously, if we could turn the time
clock back to that period in the growth and development
of the two-year institution, we would have attempted through
staff development activities to bridge the gap at an earlier
time that may have avoided some of the serious dysfunctional

activities that still plague the community college today.

Many opportunities were lost to help each of the groups with widely differing value orientations to seek a better understanding of each other's position, and even perhaps draw from each position the strengths that would have benefited the entire institution. Instead, devoid of a formal system by which the institution analyzed its needs and proceeded to bring about the changes needed for its new direction, old positions were hardened and a dual set of standards and values were incorporated into the working philosophy of the institution. Because those standards and values were not dealt with at the time the major change took place, they exist today and constitute a major barrier to the development of a unified institution.

The second significant change of the "transformational" type perhaps occurred around 1947 and was epitomized by the publication of the Truman Commission report entitled "Higher Education for American Democracy." This report and its accompanying value system called for the two-year colleges to: 1. change their name to community colleges; 2. integrate the vocational and transfer functions into a comprehensive mission to be delivered by a single institution; 3. add the community service and adult education functions to the existing purposes and give those functions high visibility; 4. dramatically extend access to postsecondary education to people never before considered eligible for college.

This "open door" philosophy set entirely new standards for matriculation, grading, counseling, and scope of programs and services. During this second major change period, the staff, program, and organizational development activities were more firmly in place and were supported by burgeoning enrollments, generous federal and staff budgets, foundation support, and most of all a missionary zeal that gave direction and a measure of unity to a system "whose time had come." During the years following the Truman commission report, "development" activities were designed to help staff members to "understand the philosophy of the community college." Universities offered courses in it, inservice programs concentrated on it, and staff developers found materials, consultants and all manner of resources available to help them bring about a transformational change in what was still a pliable institutional environment.

The focus of developmental activities over the past thirty years has been of the incremental variety. We have attempted to do better: What the new value orientation told us was "good and right." The "F" grade was dropped; students had a right to their own language; the second chance was extended to the third, fourth, fifth . . . ; teachers were given human relations instruction; we taught anything, anytime, to anyone; we were approaching the learning society. Lest you become confused, because from your "point of view" things didn't look at all that way, let me recognize that not all institutions nor all people accepted or bought into the new value orientation. Some institutions and some people were reluctant to accept the changes that were introduced into the system in 1917 regarding vocational emphasis and others were not at all in sympathy with the "comprehensive community college" philosophy that was introduced in the late '40s and early '50s. However, those charged with the responsibility of change agentry were, by and large, building their program on those philosophical pilings and the change process was definitely incremental in nature.

The values and the standards by which the community colleges were growing and developing were slowly becoming accepted by an increasingly large proportion of the people in the institutions and those in positions of power outside of it. There has never been a scarcity of critics who see dimly if at all the nature of the community college, who have taken upon themselves to chastise the institution for not being what they from their 1900 or 1920 perspective think that it ought to be. The danger for those who are in staff, program, and organizational development activities is that we too may become myopic in refusing to take that historical perspective, and may feel that the only way for development to go is the way that it has gone during our tenure in the institution, and may fail to recognize that the need for trans- formational change may be at hand.

This now brings us to the uncomfortable prospect that we may be in, or may be about to enter, a third period of changing values and standards. Kindler outlines these changing values and standards as conditions calling for a switch from incremental change strategies to transformational change strategies, as indicated by the following two conditions: "1. The environment introduces new factors (new competition, technology, or government regulations) that adversely affect productivity, satisfaction, or growth, or 2. constraints of the system are too confining to allow adequate movement toward the objectives."

There are several items that may emerge along with the Smith-Hughes Act and the Truman Commission Report as indicators of the need for a transformational change. These indicators will probably signal those in staff, program, and organizational development that our efforts are going to be focused in different directions than they have been in the past and that the "little deaths" that accompany each minor change that takes place in our personal and professional lives as we go about moving through incremental change activities are likely to be replaced by "the big one" that comes with major change.

It is our job to look, with as much accuracy as we can muster, at the indicators that have meaning to us and our institution. It is also our responsibility to design "development" activities that are capable of bringing about the changes called for in the most effective way possible. It is not by accident that the book topping the best seller's list has been the one by Peters and Waterman, *In Search of Excellence*. It is not by accident that voices like those of Terry O'Banion, the director of the League for Innovation, and Robert McCabe, president of Miami-Dade Community College, are being heard discussing excellence, standards, and a new value system to guide the community colleges during the remaining '80s, '90s and into the 21st century.

What roles should staff development people play to enable the community college to incorporate this change? Will our new push for standards and excellence be developed and implemented with the client in mind—as apparently our past policies have operated—or will the new criteria of excellence focus on what is good for the deliverer of the services—as has been the case in some other institutions?

For those of you in staff, program, and organizational development, let me offer a few suggestions. I suppose this section could be entitled "Confessions of a 'High S'* About to Embark on a Transformational Change." First, hopefully we will not confuse excellence with status, performance with reputation, nor the forfeiting of building self-esteem for the building of institutional esteem. I would like staff development people to consider carefully the application of Peters' and Waterman's eight attributes, which are distinctive of excellent and innovative companies, as perhaps having some relevance to excellence in the community college setting. Hopefully, our development activities continue to emphasize an institution's "bias for action." Many of the voices leading us in the new direction seem to be concentrating on analysis, but hopefully not at the expense of risk-taking and action.

The second attribute identified by Peters and Waterman is that of "close to the customer" which hopefully, as you go about preparing your staff development programs, you never lose sight of. The discipline should never become so important that we fail to have a concern for those who have difficulty mastering it. If your in-service programs produce master technicians but fail to maintain that caring individual in the classroom, I am not sure that achieving the "excellence" brought about by that change will be worth the effort.

Another of the attributes contained in *In Search of Excellence* is entitled "Productivity Through People." Much of our potential for excellence is unrealized because our developmental activities have not truly helped people to operate in a collaborative, supportive way. Managers fail to achieve excellence in their units because of inability or unwillingness to recognize and reward the accomplishments of the people whom they supervise. Chief executives short-change the institution because of their lack of recognition and reward behaviors for members of their management team. Teachers in the classrooms fail to provide the students with the same kind of positive reinforcement that they seek from their administrators. These are all things that can become part of the development program as we chart a

---

*A major work behavioral dimension identified by Dr. John G. Geier (University of Minnesota) labeled as "steadiness or sitability" and characterized by loyalty, family orientation, possessiveness, great concern with security, and a disposition of slowness to change.

course toward excellence.

The last attribute taken from the Peters and Waterman book still appears to me to be the most critical aspect of future development programs—that being the establishment of a value system by which the institution is governed. While we may only be dealing with semantics, it might be most important that we consider carefully "raising expectations, not standards." Standards, if improperly implemented, can become the most unfair and unproductive of all practices. Standards might put ceilings on expectations and for students capable of that "creative leap" they may create a siren song to only "meet the standard." For students unable to meet the "standard," they may provide the final crushing blow to any self-esteem still harbored by that individual. Standards invite comparisons between people rather than encouraging each individual to become all he is capable of becoming. While none of these conditions are inherent in the application of standards by themselves, it behooves staff development people to place them in a context where they actually contribute to the development of excellence in its most positive form.

Change agentry at this critical point in the development of the community college system will not be easy, but perhaps by looking back at other times when transformational changes were called for and learning from our historical successes and mistakes, people in staff, program, and organizational development can be major contributors in bringing about the new transformational change.

ABOUT THE AUTHOR

VERNON R. PICKETT is President of
Lower Columbia College in Longview,
Washington. This former high school counselor and history instructor has been a professional educator for more than 25 years.
After receiving his doctorate in educational
administration, he was one of a nucleus of
persons who founded Kirkwood Community
College in Cedar Rapids, Iowa.

3
Focusing on
the "Right" Questions

Vernon R. Pickett

Community colleges increasingly are being asked for assistance in helping communities and states across our nation to effectively cope with the changes occurring in the social, economic, and political sectors of American society.[1] Concurrently, community colleges are faced with stresses and forces arising out of demographic, financial, and technological changes which pose major challenges to their ways of doing business. Crucial to their success in responding effectively to these expectations and forces will be the ability of their leaders—administrative, faculty, and trustees—to focus attention on key questions and issues. The questions and issues go beyond the more immediate concerns for enrollment, finance, and technology to matters of educational purpose, quality, and vitality.

The concerns on which community college educators are focusing their attention today are somewhat different than they were a few brief years ago. During the heady days of the 1960s and 1970s, the issues centered on increasing enrollments, providing access, employing faculty, and building buildings. The public provided the colleges with relatively uncritical support. It permitted them, for the most part, to define their mission and programs locally within broad parameters established by the state.

In more recent years, a shift has occurred. Many colleges now are experiencing declining enrollments, increasing financial constraints, retrenching of staff, cutting back of programs and services, encroachment on local control, and a more critical posture on the part of the public towards education. Keller (1983) described many of these new forces in terms of: (1) the changing demography of students in higher education, e.g., declining numbers; shifts in racial, ethnic, and cultural backgrounds; increasing age; and growth in the number of part-time students; (2) the disintegration of the liberal arts curriculum; (3) the growing competition among colleges for students and faculty; (4) the impact of technology on how colleges conduct their work and their ability to respond to the needs of business and industry; (5) the challenge of maintaining faculty excellence and loyalty in the face of changing compensation patterns and institutional expectations of faculty role; and (6) the growing dominance of outside controls at the expense of local autonomy.[2]

Additional forces are at work which also are impacting community colleges. They emanate from basic changes which are occurring in our society. Naisbett (1982) describes them in terms of shifts from (1) an industrial to an information society, (2) forced technology to high tech/high touch, (3) a national to world economy, (4) a short-term to a long-term orientation, (5) centralization to decentralization in government and organizations, (6) representative to participatory democracy, (7) institutional to self help, (8) organizations based on hierarchical structure to those based on networking forms, (9) north to south, and (10) single to multiple options.[3]

Whether or not one agrees with Naisbett's view of the future, there seems little doubt that American society is undergoing profound changes and that education's role is substantial in helping others to analyze, understand, interpret, and prepare for these changes. Drucker (1983) points this out in the context of the shift to an information-based society. He observes that the fundamental element in ensuring productivity is people's knowledge and skills; and these, in turn, are a product of the education provided by the schools. He concludes that the schools will respond effectively to this challenge because society will accept no less.[4]

Thus, we have a multiplicity of forces impacting on community colleges—some which focus on enrollments, finance, facilities, compensation, and governance and which tend to be of a more immediate, specific, operational nature; and others emanating from major societal changes of a social, economic, and political nature, which are of a relatively long-range and general type. Obviously, community college educators must deal with both types of forces. A major point of this article is that they must be especially concerned, however, to give adequate attention to the implications arising out of the second set of forces.

The role of presidents in focusing their colleges' attention on the educational implications of these forces is based on the premises that the most effective leaders have a clear vision of where their institutions are going, and that they effectively communicate this to other members of their organizations. They set forth a limited number of goals, and they mobilize the resources of their organizations toward their achievement. They maintain relatively high visibility for the purpose of staying in touch with what's going on, and they constantly reinforce the essential values and goals they envision for their organizations.[5]

What presidents and other college leaders choose to focus their attention on tends to define the questions and priorities toward which the participants in the educational enterprise— faculty, administrators, and trustees—will direct their efforts. Community colleges, in the face of financial constraints and declining enrollments, must be careful not to develop a short-term survival mentality, dealing only with operational issues. Institution by institution, they must devote enough time and energy to the strategic component of management, seeking answers to such questions as: "What are we educating people for?" "How well must we do it?" and "How do we stay abreast of change and implement and adapt to it as educators and collegiate institutions?" The remainder of this article will consider the preceding three questions in greater detail from a president's perspective. In so doing, it focuses on the role of the president; but, it applies to all college leaders, administrative, faculty, and trustees alike.

First, presidents should focus their attention and the attention of their colleagues on the question, "What are we educating people for?" This question deals with the purpose and substance of education in the community college. Presidents should ensure that the right questions are being asked, and answers sought, regarding the most appropriate kind of education, given the changes which are occurring in the work place, community, nation, and world. For example, in the transition from a manufacturing-based economy to an information-based one, people need to acquire new skills in order to become or to remain productive. But they also need to be helped to understand the major societal changes themselves and the implications and options which arise accordingly. A whole new set of issues and problems will emerge if the information society results in the demise of the middle class, as some writers fear.[6]

What is the responsibility of community colleges to help students and the people in the communities they serve to understand these options and possibilities? More and more people are finding their work skills are no longer needed; and yet, even with retraining, the opportunities for work are very limited in some communities and areas of our nation. Therefore, should the colleges give more attention to entrepreneurial studies; or to acquiring basic learning skills in reading, writing, and math? In view of the inexorable move to a technology-based society where the products of technology can so readily and easily be used for the enhancement or degradation of humankind, what emphases should be given to helping students and the nonstudent citizens in college communities understand the value-based decision options which exist regarding the use of technology? Where does each college stand regarding the place of liberal education in its curriculum, given the highly transitory nature of community college students? How can "liberating" concepts be built into the curriculum on a discipline basis? Should there be an integrated, common core of courses which all students take?

We know that educators in community colleges, by
choice or by default, will answer these questions and many
more regarding the purposes and content of education. The
responsibility of those who lead is to ensure that the questions are being asked and answers are being sought in a
thoughtful, purposeful way.

Second, presidents should cause their institutions to
focus on the question, "Are we educating our students well
enough?" In recent months, the quality of education has
become a national concern and a major political issue. A
number of reports have been issued decrying the inadequacy
of quality in our schools and colleges. This issue is not likely
to go away soon.

Drucker (1983) puts the concern for quality into perspective. He notes that productivity determines the ability of
employers to pay. Ultimately, it determines the real incomes
of people. He concludes that, because productivity in an
information-based economy is much more dependent on the
knowledge and skills of its workers than was the case in a
manufacturing-based economy, the success of our schools in
developing the knowledge and skills required is more critical
today than ever before.[7]

As community colleges focus on the quality issue, they
must be careful not to confuse quality and standards. Standards do not guarantee quality. In defining excellence,
the National Commission on Excellence in Education (1983)
provides a useful definition of quality. For the individual
learner, the commission defines excellence as ". . . perfor-
ming on the boundary of individual ability in ways that test
and push back personal limits, in school and in the work
place. Excellence characterizes a school or college that sets
high expectations and goals for all learners, then tries in
every way possible to help students reach them."[8]

Standards, on the other hand, refer to predetermined
levels of acceptable performance, but they do not *necessarily*
imply any connection between performance and individual
ability nor the obligation to try in every way possible to
help students to reach acceptable performance levels once
the levels have been established.

The commission's definition implies that causing individual learners to perform in ways that extend their per-

sonal limits *commensurate* with their abilities is an essential characteristic of quality in teaching and programs. Likewise, it recognizes the importance not only of setting high expectations but also the corollary responsibility to make every possible effort to help students to attain them. Thus, quality in teaching cannot be determined apart from progress in learning. Further, the college's responsibility to breathe life into ". . . every way possible . . ." through proper support for teaching and learning cannot be escaped.

Presidents should encourage faculty and administrators to focus their attention on the adequacy and appropriateness of the college's expectations regarding performance. Are the expectations appropriate, given the students' goals, the expectations of the community, and the changing requirements of society? Is enough being expected of students? Is sufficient attention being given to individual differences among students and to their progress in learning? Is proper support being provided so that students can achieve at expected levels and teachers can provide the experiences needed? Once again, the questions are many. What is essential is that those persons in leadership positions communicate to faculty, administrators, and students the importance of being actively engaged in defining, determining, and maintaining quality education.

A third question on which the attention of presidents and their colleagues needs to be focused is, "How do we, as educators and educational institutions, stay abreast of, implement, and adapt to change?" What must be done for colleges to engage in continuous renewal? Their ability to remain innovative, to change in meaningful and productive ways over time is crucial to continued vitality and effectiveness.

A key to maintaining vitality and innovation rests in the ability of people in organizations to grow and remain actively engaged in their work. As a result of their study, Peters and Waterman (1982) observe that excellent companies are characterized by an ability to incorporate change in their organizations and to respond to changes in their environments. The people in these companies share in common a respect for others. This respect is extended to all employees, including those who work at the lowest levels in the firms, whose ideas and feelings are actively sought and seriously considered by senior-level management. The leadership of these companies effectively instills in their work forces a strong sense of the firms' values. The values vary from one company to the next, but within each there is consensus regarding which values are most important. All of the companies in this study place a high priority on training for their employees, and all of these firms have a record of vitality, innovation, and growth over an extended period of time.[9]

What can we learn about organizational renewal from this study? We learn that the role of senior-level leadership is crucial. Effective leaders focus their organization's attention on a few goals and shared values. They respect people at all levels of the organizational hierarchy and their contributions to their firm's success. Strategies and mechanisms are created to ensure that this attitude of respect is communicated and the contributions offered are valued. Time and energy are committed to the development of skills and knowledge of employees, who are then given considerable authority and latitude within which to accomplish their work.

Strategic planning, with its emphasis on institutional mission, a short- to medium-range time orientation, and external environments is a means by which many colleges are are staying close to the changes which are impacting or are likely to impact them. Baldridge and Okimi (1982) view the central focus of strategic planning as ". . . developing a good fit between the organization's activities and the demands of surrounding environments."[10] As such, it provides a means for maintaining a dynamic relationship between colleges and their changing environments. Strategic planning encourages drawing on the expertise of people from all parts of an organization and applying this expertise to specific tasks and problems on a real-time basis. Consequently, properly conceived and executed, it can be a useful tool for helping colleges and their employees to grow and change and to retain their vitality and effectiveness over time.

Ensuring that colleges maintain a capability to renew themselves involves the shaping of attitudes. Presidents need to stress their respect for all employees and to encourage others to do so as well. Attention needs to be given to developing strategies and mechanisms by which the ideas and views of persons at all levels can be expressed in meaningful ways. Resources need to be committed so that all employees may perceive a willing support for them in acquiring and maintaining the skills they need to do their jobs well.

A hallmark of effective leaders is their ability to focus on the "right" questions. In the face of major changes which American society is undergoing, and shifting pressures impacting community colleges, community college leaders must strike a balance between the more immediate operational concerns which their institutions face and the more global societal ones to which the colleges are being asked to respond. Both types of concerns are important and must be dealt with; but, in times of fiscal constraints, declining enrollments, and retrenching of staff, pressures are strong to focus almost exclusively on these problems. It is especially important at just these times that community college presidents and other college leaders focus adequate attention on questions of educational purpose and quality and institutional vitality and adaptability. In so doing, the responsibility which community colleges have to assist their constituents in acquiring the necessary knowledge, skills, and values to cope effectively with the changing American society is most likely to be properly fulfilled.

REFERENCES

[1] American Association of Community and Junior Colleges. 1983 "Governors Brief." *AACJC Letter*. 23 August, No. 55.

[2] Keller, G. 1983 *Academic Strategy: The Management Revolution in American Higher Education*. John Hopkins University Press: pp. 12-26.

[3] Naisbett, J. 1982 *Megatrends: Ten New Directions Transforming Our Lives*. Warner Books: p. 290.

[4] Drucker, P. 1983 *The Wall Street Journal*. 19 July.

[5] Peters, T. J., Waterman, R. H. 1982 *In Search of Excellence*. Harper and Row: pp. 235-291.

[6] Kuttner, B. 1983 "The Declining Middle." *The Atlantic Monthly*. July: pp. 60-72.

[7] Drucker, P. 1983 *The Wall Street Journal*. 19 July.

[8]The National Commission on Excellence in Education. 1983 *A Nation at Risk: The Imperative for Educational Reform.* April: p. 12.

[9]Peters, T. J., Waterman, R. H. 1982 *In Search of Excellence.* Harper and Row: pp. 235-291.

[10]Baldridge, J. V., Okimi, P. H. 1982 "Strategic Planning in Higher Education: New Tool—or New Gimmick?" *AAHE Bulletin.* October: pp. 6-18.

ABOUT THE AUTHOR

NEAL A. NORRIS is a futurist educator
with a Doctor of Education degree who presently holds the position of Coordinator of
Curriculum Development at Reading Area
Community College in Reading, Pennsyl-
vania. This member of NCSPOD's Future
Trends Commission is also a member of the
Center for Global Perspectives in Education,
the World Future Society, and a co-founder
of the Connecticut Organization for Professional Development. Norris is a former
coordinator of the Connecticut Teacher
Center Network, editor of the "Futures
Information Interchange," member of the
Gifted and Talented Planning Team for the
state of Connecticut, and a presenter at the
Third Annual World Future Society Education Section Conference.

4

The Community College as a Future-Oriented Community Learning System

Neal A. Norris

> If, (a) the future is to be different from the past, and if (b) we are to live our lives in the future, then (c) we ought to educate for a changed future—one different from the present or the past.
>
> William F. Ogburn, 1935

INTRODUCTION

In 1953 the Indian thinker, Jiddu Krishnamurti, offered this penetrating insight into the relationship between the nature of education and the significance of life:

> When one travels around the world, one notices to what an extraordinary degree human nature is the same, whether in India or America, in Europe or Australia. This is especially true in colleges and universities. We are turning out, as if through a mould, a type of human being whose chief interest is to find security, to become somebody important, or to have a good time with as little thought as possible.
>
> Conventional education makes independent thinking extremely difficult. Conformity leads to mediocrity. To be different from the group or to resist environment is not easy and is often risky as long as we worship success. The urge to

be successful, which is the pursuit of reward whether in the
material or in the so-called spiritual sphere, the search for
inward or outward security, the desire for comfort—this
whole process smothers discontent, puts an end to spontaneity
and breeds fear; and fear blocks the intelligent understanding
of life. With increasing age, dullness of mind and heart sets in.

In seeking comfort, we generally find a quiet corner in life
where there is a minimum of conflict, and then we are afraid
to step out of that seclusion. This fear of life, this fear of
struggle and of new experience, kills in us the spirit of adven-
ture; our whole upbringing and education have made us afraid
to be different from our neighbor, afraid to think contrary to
the established pattern of society, falsely respectful of authority and tradition.

. . . Now, what is the significance of life? What are we
living and struggling for? If we are being educated merely to
achieve distinction, to get a better job, to be more efficient,
to have wider domination over others, then our lives will be
shallow and empty. If we are being educated only to be
scientists, to be scholars wedded to books, or specialists ad-
dicted to knowledge, then we shall be contributing to the
destruction and misery of the world.

Though there *is* a higher and wider significance to life,
of what value is our education if we never discover it? We may
be highly educated, but if we are without deep integration of
thought and feeling, our lives are incomplete, contradictory
and torn with many fears; and as long as education does not
cultivate an integrated outlook on life, it has very little significance.[1]

Today—almost a third of a century later—the contemporary characteristics of this relationship have again captured
the attention of parents, students, educators, politicians,
and citizens alike. Perhaps the political thinker, Sheldon
Wolin, identified one essential, yet problematic, feature of
this relationship for Americans when he noted:

The problem is that by its own self-understanding science
is inherently incapable of serving society as other great political and religious world views have in the past. Science is a
source neither of moral renewal nor of political vision; it has
no principle that requires solicitude for traditions or historical
identities that, until recently, were the basis for most political
thinking and action. There is still time to deal with this problem before the memory of democracy and education is ob-
literated, but it requires a clearer picture of the stakes and
their form.

Democracy is being incorporated into higher education

at a time when education itself is becomming more completely integrated into the needs of a political and economic system that is struggling to compete in the changing international political economy. Given the strategic importance of scientific and technical training in this setting, the consequences for the future of democracy are profoundly disturbing. Education for a scientific society will reproduce yet again the two-tiered system that has characterized the history of American education, only this time it will take the form of advanced scientific education for the few and a technical education for the many. The specific nature of a technical education is that it is what it claims to be, immediately useful. The technician, in other words, is a unit of potential power, ready to be fitted into the predesigned slot for which his or her education has been a preparation. It is at this point that the demise of liberal and humanistic education becomes crucial. As more and more educational time is taken up with technical subjects to the exclusion of humanistic ones, the individual becomes a more "perfect" unit of power, unalloyed by useless, reflective, critical notions of the kind deposited by the humanities, and hence easily integrated into the system as a whole person, that is, a person who is only the sum of his/her technical parts. . . . The problem does not require a simple restoration of a humanities curriculum, but a facing up to the fact that if current tendencies in higher education go unchallenged, then higher education will continue to be an essential cornerstone of the antidemocratic structure of our society.[2]

Some of the implications of these current tendencies have not entirely escaped concerned educators, as evidenced by the recent spate of national commission reports, government studies, and scholarly projects.[3] With certain notable exceptions, most of these works have failed to recognize the full magnitude, intricate complexity, and profound consequences of our present position in history.[4]

OVERVIEW OF THE FUTURIST RATIONALE

Futurists have attempted to provide such meta-analysis of this issue and to offer a variety of solutions based on their analyses. It is possible to construct a highly generalized hypothetical futurist rationale from the strands of futurist thinking that appear in the work of futurists and their organizations. Two fundamental aspects comprise this hypothetical futurist rationale: a view of the present global situation of humanity and a view of possible ways of resolving that situation. Futurists have achieved a relative consensus regarding the characteristic features of the current situation while the numerous solutions they provide vary enormously.

The futurist critique of contemporary American education is based on futurist views of global socio-historical development, particularly in the West. Many futurists appear to conceptualize history in terms of a few fundamentally important socio-cultural developmental stages and transitional eras.

Most futurists agree that the transitional nature of the present socio-cultural situation is a rare occurrence of critical importance. The modern era is often characterized as a turning point, transformation, or breakpoint which has occurred only one or two times previously throughout history. Our era is compared to the great transition from nomadic existence in paleolithic and mesolithic time to agricultural existence during neolithic times, and to the transition from the neolithic agricultural village to urban civilization around 3000 B.C.[5] Many futurists also argue that the current transitional era is a unique and critical phase of human development. Successful navigation of this period depends on a fundamental restructuring of individual and societal values within a very short period of time. Otherwise human catastrophe is quite probable if not inevitable.

The achievement of the current stage of socio-cultural development required the acceptance by almost all Western societies of a world-view (and image of the future) built upon positivistic naturalism validated through empirical science.[6] This world-view has had both positive and negative consequences. First, the rate of scientific discovery and technological innovation has accelerated more rapidly in the last century, tremendously enlarging humanity's technical capacity to influence its outer and inner environments. This power has grown at a faster pace than the moral, ethical, and spiritual development of the human species, overcoming individual and collective capacities to comprehend sufficiently and use wisely these expanded technical powers. The unforeseen and little understood psycho-social implications of these expanded technical capacities has created problems of unprecedented magnitude, complexity, and interrelation which are approaching critical proportions and may soon reach the point of no return.

Many futurists recognize that humanity now has the power to destroy itself physically and spiritually. Most also recognize the fragility of the biosphere. The concept of the interdependence of ecosystems has been transferred to the arena of human relations through the emphasis placed on the interdependence of the numerous races and national states throughout the world.

A second consequence of Western humanity's increased technical capacities, especially in communications, transportation, production, and biochemistry, has been the sharing of certain historical experiences and trends. Two world wars and the Great Depression highlight global trends toward increased industrialization, urbanization, Westernization, institutional bureaucratization, and socialization of education and war.

These developments have lead to the recognition that the meaning of the human condition must now be reconsidered. While many futurists would accept much of this description of the global situation, they would emphasize different reasons for its occurrence and promote various means of successfully reaching the next stage of socio-cultural development.

Neither the diagnostic nor prescriptive elements of the futurist rationale are unique. What is important about futurist thinking is that it often adopts a holistic perspective from which to view these elements and emphasizes the fundamental role education plays in negotiating the current transitional era. That perspective has been organized in different ways by each wing of the futurist field.

Scientific-technological futurists take an approach to the future emanating from a control and management orientation. They seek to ease the stress and dislocation generated by the present situation by controlling future events through the use of sophisticated forecasting techniques integrated by a comprehensive cybernetic systems theory.

While recognizing that the technological applications of various scientific discoveries have had some significant detrimental consequences, the scientific-technological futurists remain faithful to the essence of the prevailing Western world-view. They presume that the solution to whatever problems are caused can be found by creating newer, more potent technologies. Social futurists (the activist arm of scientific-technological futurism) such as Alvin Toffler, employ a democratic decision-making model based on systematic anticipation of potential problems and wide participation in their resolution.

Visionary-alternatives futurists use a wide variety of heuristic approaches as a way of creating rather than controlling the future. Images of the future are of great importance to these futurists, especially those images embodied in adapted versions of general systems theory and in the various spiritual fusions of science and art.

THE FUTURIST EDUCATIONAL CRITIQUE

Educational historians have recognized that the most recent educational reform movement (beginning in the late 1950s and continuing through the mid-1970s) differed from previous educational reform movements since it lacked a specific focus. Instead, reformers nurtured a broad range of reforms aimed at the structure and content of education.[7]

The euphoria of that reform period has now faded, and most critics agree that education in the 1980s is beset by a number of unprecedented conditions. The chief visible symptoms of the present educational context include: increasing absenteeism, violence, disciplinary concerns, and factionalization among professional and interest groups; decreasing federal, state, and local funding; and fading optimism. The prevailing diagnosis of these critics is that the system is now critically ill, and the prognosis is more uncertain than ever before.

Most critics have substantially neglected two aspects of the futurist rationale: the pivotal importance ascribed to knowledge and to education.[8] Daniel Bell, Herman Kahn, and other futurists have defined education instrumentally, and understand it primarily as "intellectual technology." The chief purpose of education for these futurists is to mediate the creation, legitimization, and transmission of increasingly theoretical and technical information among knowledge elites within government, business, the military, and academe. Education should prepare the required number of systems engineers, technicians, planners, and global citizens to fill the highly specialized, meritocratic occupational system of a technology laden post-industrial society. Knowledge and occupation would be mediated through the system of education, and a large portion of the burden would fall on the universities.

At the end of his introduction to *The Coming of Post Industrial Society*, Daniel Bell disclosed the real purpose of his work:

> What I am arguing in this book is that the major source of structural change in society—the change in the modes of innovation in the relation of science to technology and in public policy—is the change in the character of knowledge: the exponential growth and branching of science, the rise of a new intellectual technology, the creation of systematic research through R and D budgets, and, as the calyx of all this, the codification of theoretical knowledge.[9]

The implicit one-dimensionality of education within the post-industrial society described by Bell and Kahn was vividly depicted by Peter Drucker in an exquisite historical analogy:

> There is a horrible example in history of what the Educated Society might easily become unless the university commits itself to the education of the whole man. It is the destruction of one of the world's greatest and most creative civilizations, the China of T'ang and Sung periods, by the imposition of a purely verbal, purely intellectual, purely analytical education on man and society, the Confucian Canon. Within a century, this commitment to the purely intellectual in man destroyed what had been the world's leader in art as well as in science, in technology as well as in philosophy. We are today in a similar danger—for we, too, tend, under the impact of the triumphs of organization and of the analytical mind, to downgrade everything that is direct, immediate and not verbal.[10]

Knowledge and education are also fundamental in visionary-alternatives futurist thinking. Most of these futurists view knowledge as evolutionary rather than accumulative, and define education as broadly transcendent.[11] Its overriding purpose is to promote individual and societal transformation. Education would link physics to metaphysics and create a new epistomological understanding.[12]

Though very different views concerning educational purposes, structures, and strategies are depicted, the fundamental importance of education as a basic means of negotiating the transition and resolving "the mentality problem" is adopted by many futurists in both wings of the field.

If the United States and other advanced industrial societies are involved in a critically important transitional era as futurists maintain, and if individual attitudes and perceptions are lagging farther and farther behind ongoing scientific and technological developments, then some means of closing that gap quickly appears necessary. Futurists have usually been harsh in their criticism of the confining structure and obsolete content of contemporary education; nevertheless, they continue to place great faith in its ability to "bridge the human gap" and resolve "the world problematique."[13]

Futurists have questioned a multitude of educational practices and provided a fundamental challenge to transform education comprised of five characteristic features: (1) a definition of education that moves beyond the confines of conventional schooling, (2) reconceptualized organizational patterns, (3) a reformulated curriculum, (4) a new configuration of instructional methods, and (5) the infusion of available and emerging technologies. *Futurists criticize educators for their archaic structures, teaching strategies, and perceptions. They claim education has been far too rigidly conceived, organized, and transacted.*

Futurists often argue that the imperialism of formal education within conventional schools—perpetuating a cluster of practices based more on tradition and conventional wisdom than on solid research and evaluation—has shackled education to parochial interests and obsolete mythologies. Futurist educators contend the traditional institutional context of education composed of conventional schooling arrangements organized in age-graded structural and curricular patterns, is obsolete in advanced industrial societies in which technologies of unprecedented scope and depth are being rapidly diffused.

Futurists point to the lack of options within the conventional system as a fundamental weakness. Since the structure, content, methods, and results of the current educational enterprise are obsolete, these cannot help but be unresponsive and insensitive to the needs of individuals, communities, and the species as a whole. They argue that revolutionary developments in electronics, communications, data processing, and bio-genetics will force a tremendous expansion in how education is conceived. Soon it will span all ages and will be decentralized in space and time to permit diverse organizational patterns that meet individual needs.

The move from conventional schooling arrangements to life-long living-learning systems responsive to individual needs and concerns should begin immediately futurists argue. This educational tranformation requires new organizational patterns and expansion of the legitimate ways of learning. It will be mediated by potent new electronic, bio-genetic, and medical technologies (i.e., silicon-based intelligences such as sophisticated robots and thinking androids, synergistic human computer symbiosis, genetic transformation of the brain and of human nature and anti-aging and memory enhancement pills).

Futurists contend these emerging technologies should be introduced into education as one way of tranforming the structure of schooling. Computer-assisted, managed, and mediated learning should be encouraged, as should two-way interactive television, micro-computers and other silicon based intelligence systems.

In short, futurists have presumed that the contemporary constitution of American education is irrelevant, anachronistic, and obsolete when viewed in relation to emerging global realities and critical transitional concerns.

This necessary refiguration of education ideally requires a simultaneous assault on educational theory and practice, which some futurists believe can occur. Others have adopted a more pragmatic transformational process in which (1) all aspects of the primary educational institutions (i.e., the schools and school districts) are substantially reconstructed, and (2) these conventional institutional and organizational patterns are then transcended on the way toward developing decentralized, individualized life-long living-learning systems.

Key aspects of this process include greater community participation, increased programmatic options, and humane recognition and humanistic application of emerging educational technologies to enhance the decentralized, parti-

cipatory, individualized features that should characterize
life-long learning in a post-industrial society.

FUTURIST EDUCATIONAL PRESCRIPTIONS
AND THE COMMUNITY COLLEGE

Futurist educators like Alvin Toffler; Harold Shane;
Ronald Barnes; Donald Glines; and James Bowman, Christopher Dede, Frederick Kierstead, and John Pulliam have
prescribed various remedies for the critically ill educational
system. These futurists view education as a central, essentially transformative agency within society. The scope of
this paper does not allow a comprehensive presentation of
their educational prescriptions. Each has recognized the
unique position and potential of the community college within an overall living and learning system and should be studied
in detail.[14] A brief summary of chief futurist prescriptions is
necessary to provide a framework within which staff, program, and organizational development practitioners can construct their own future-oriented work.

Alvin Toffler, in his book *Learning for Tomorrow*, urged
educators to redefine learning as a process of enlarging,
enriching, and improving the individual's image of the future.
He felt learners should learn to cope with real-life crises,
opportunities, and perils. This could be accomplished by
future-orienting education based on action-learning concepts and decision-making skills.[15]

Harold Shane argued that education should become more
humane, personalized, and process-oriented. Since learning is
a continuous and life-long process, education should also become continuous and life-long. He proposed a "seamless
curriculum continuum" that would promote: (1) year-round
schooling; (2) flexible scheduling; (3) team teaching; (4)
personalized educational experiences; and (5) psychologically
supportive nurturance of self-identity, self-orientation, and
self-direction.[16]

Donald Glines felt the chief task for educators should be
to assist and lead society through the global transition; the
primary goal should be to create a preferable future world;
and the basic approach should be small-scale and option
oriented. To accomplish this task of reformulating education,

Glines argued that all aspects of the school—philosophy, instruction, learning, structure, technology, and reporting—should be reorganized simultaneously. He proposed the creation of four program options to replace the conventional school program and provided a detailed description of an actual example (The Wilson Campus School) applying these proposals.[17]

Ronald Barnes proposed one of the most comprehensive future-oriented educational prescriptions in the early 1970s when he helped design a Learning System for the proposed Minnesota Experimental City. Access to the MXC Learning System would be through the Disorientation/Orientation/Reorientation Center. This center would assist the learner to: (1) view himself as an active participant rather than a passive recipient in the learning process, (2) recognize that learning was his responsibility, (3) realize that learning how to learn is most important, and (4) become self-reliant.

Other components of the proposed MXC Learning System included: (1) a computer network information access system; (2) the caring relationship developed between resource persons and the learner; (3) an array of available tools and equipment; and (4) several multi-use facilities such as (a) Beginning Life Centers, (b) Stimulus Centers, (c) Gaming Centers, (d) Project Centers, (e) Learner Banks, and (f) Family-Life Centers.[18]

Bowman, Dede, Kierstead, and Pulliam, arguing from what they termed the "pragmatic/reconstructionist" educational philosophy, contended the goals of education should be cultural transformation and initiation of shared visions of the future. These goals would be accomplished by organizing communication-era education around four Problem Analysis/Futures Planning Centers: (1) Priority Centers, (2) Community Centers, (3) National Centers, and (4) Global Centers.[19]

Futurist criticism of contemporary American educational theory and practice indicates that significant changes are required to provide relevant learning opportunities to today's students. Futurist educators have created several prescriptive models that provide appropriate alternatives to present educational practices. Each model is designed around new ways of understanding the relationship between knowledge and learning. Most proposed alternative learning systems include a substantially reformulated curriculum design reflecting the characteristic features of the larger system.

Futurist educators would reverse the prevailing emphasis on scientific and technological approaches to curriculum making. They often emphasize seven characteristic features of an effective educational program. First, it should provide several options to the conventional educational program. Second, it should span traditional disciplinary boundaries to inter-relate knowledge from all fields. Third, it should focus on and respond to critical problems of the real world. Fourth, it should be concerned with the imagination, design, and realization of alternative futures as well as understanding of the present and past. Fifth, it should include a global and cosmic as well as local and national perspectives. Sixth, it should emphasize ways of learning rather than strategies of teaching. And seventh, it should be sensitive to individual needs and be concerned with the exploration, realization, and expansion of human potential.

THE EMERGING POTENTIAL OF CREATING A FUTURE-ORIENTED LEARNING SYSTEM

The general futurist rationale, educational critique, and selected prescriptions should offer a unique perspective from which to consider the unprecedented opportunities now available to community, junior, and technical college educators. Today, we confront an educational challenge of greater magnitude and more profound consequences than that of providing "free, universal, and public" education to the masses of Americans during the early decades of the 20th Century. The facts are staggering and speak for themselves. In 1900, American colleges and universities enrolled only about 200,000 students; in 1981, almost 10 million people— more than one-third of whom were over 25 years of age— registered as students within institutions of higher education.

The traditional configuration of higher education in the United States is also changing dramatically. American business and industry has become heavily involved in their own massive educational and training efforts, spending between 80 and 100 billion dollars a year. American Telephone and

Telegraph alone spends almost 1.3 billion dollars on employee training. A massive market for full and part-time educators has opened in these areas, providing approximately 700,000 positions.

As "sunset" industries, such as steel, shipbuilding, textiles, and auto, fade from predominance, efforts to retrain laid-off workers and obtain those with the new skills required by the "sunrise" industries (i.e., computer, electronics, telecommunications, aerospace, pharmaceutical, biogenetic, etc.) will escalate significantly. The stakes are global and the options we devise and initiate will substantially determine the effectiveness with which our society will negotiate the current transitional epoch.[20]

The community college occupies a unique position within the postsecondary field of education. As Marvin Feldman has noted, the community college is "one of the great social inventions of the industrial era."[21] The characteristic mission, flexibility, responsiveness, and option-orientation of the community college have combined in a fashion that has resulted in what is widely recognized as the most vibrant segment of higher education today. To retain the capacity to respond imaginatively, community college educators must accept a leadership role in identifying and incorporating "new opportunities for diversity."[22] To accomplish this, we must:

1. Unlearn the conventional controlling assumptions and predominant configuration of 20th century higher education;

2. Devise an option-oriented curriculum that provides a dynamic balance between the humane arts and occupational studies;

3. Construct multiple approaches to learning and teaching that are sensitive to diverse ages and needs of our students and colleagues;

4. Emphasize specific areas of strength, including capacities to provide enhanced accessibility to—as well as appropriate opportunities for—continuing, life-long education; and

5. Seek a shared sense of educational purpose and vision

grounded in a more comprehensive understanding of our present position in history and the strength of human choice.

As educators, our goal could then become the conceptualization and organization of a future-oriented community learning system—one which included as a matter of course—such characteristic features as long-range planning, comprehensive professional support services, option-oriented ways of learning, and an educational agenda that encouraged a fundamental concern for the significance of life.

REFERENCES

[1] Krishnamurti, Jiddu 1981 *Education and the Significance of Life.* Harper and Row, San Francisco.

[2] Wolin, S. S. 1981 "Higher Education and the Politics of Knowledge." *democrary.* 1:52.

[3] In addition to the frequently cited National Commission "A Nation at Risk" and *The Global 2000 Report*, see: The Carnegie Foundation. 1983 *The Condition of Teaching: A State-by-State Analysis.* Princeton University Press, Lawrenceville; The Carnegie Council on Policy Studies in Higher Education 1980 *Three Thousand Futures: The Next Twenty Years for Higher Education*, 1st edn. Jossey-Bass, San Francisco; Seitz, F. et al. 1982 *Outlook for Science and Technology: The Next Five Years.* W. H. Freeman and Co., San Francisco; Brown, L. R. 1981 *Building a Sustainable Society.* W. W. Norton and Co., New York; and Goodlad, J. I. et al. 1979 *A Study of Schooling.* Technical Report No. 1, Laboratory in School and Community Education, Graduate School of Education, University of California, Los Angeles.

[4] See Norris, N. A. 1982 "Educating Toward Tomorrow: A Rationale for Introducing Futurism into the Secondary School Social Studies Curriculum." Unpublished Ed.D. dissertation, School of Education, University of Massachusetts, especially chapters three and four.

[5] Boulding, K. 1965 *The Meaning of the Twentieth Century.* Harper and Row, New York; and, Polak, F. 1973 *The Image of the Future.* Jossey-Bass, San Francisco.

[6] Smith, H. 1979 "Excluded Knowledge: A Critique of the Modern Western Mind Set." *Teachers College Record.* 80:419-45; and, Smith, H. 1981 "Beyond the Western Mind Set." *Teachers College Record.* 82:434-58.

[7] Tyack, D. B., Kirst, M. W., Hansot, E. 1980 "Educational Reform: Retrospect and Prospect." *Teachers College Record.* 81:254.

[8] The relative status accorded empirically-grounded technical knowledge or spiritually-grounded imaginative insight has provided the epistomological cornerstone on which many elements of the futurist rationale are often constructed.

[9] Bell, D. 1973 *The Coming of Post-Industrial Society: A Venture in Social Forecasting.* Basic Books, New York: p. 44.

[10] Drucker, P. F. 1965 "The Rise in Higher Education." In Ford, T. (ed) *The Revolutionary Theme in Contemporary America.* Lexington: pp. 93-4.

[11] See especially the works of William Irwin Thompson and Theodore Rozak.

[12] See Thompson, W. I. and Rozak, T. Also, Capra, F. 1975 *The Tao of Physics.* Shambhala, Berkeley; and, Capra, F. 1983 *The Turning Point: Science, Society, and the Rising Culture.* Bantam, New York.

[13] Botkin, J. W., Elmandjra, M., Malitza, M. 1979 *No Limits to Learning: Bridging the Human Gap.* Pergaman Press, Oxford.

[14] See Toffler, A. (ed) 1974 *Learning for Tomorrow: The Role of the Future of Education.* Vintage Books, New York; Shane, H. G. 1977 *Curriculum Change Toward the 21st Century.* National Education Association, Washington. D.C.; Shane, H. G. 1973 *The Educational Significance of the Future.* Phi Delta Kappa, Bloomington; Barnes, R. E. 1973 *Design Strategy Statement on Education, Preliminary Report.* Preface to volume 5, part 4; Barnes, R. E. 1972 *Learning Systems for the Future.* Phi Delta Kappa Educational Foundation, Bloomington; Glines, D. E. 1978 *Educational Futures III: Change and Reality.* Anvil Press, Millville, MN; and, Bowman, J., Kierstead, F., Chris, D., Pulliam, J. 1978 *The Far Side of the Future: Social Problems and Educational Reconstruction.* Education Section of The World Future Society.

[15] Toffler, A. (ed) 1974 *Learning for Tomorrow: The Role of the Future of Education.* Vintage Books, New York.

[16] Shane, H. G. 1973 *The Educational Significance of the Future.* Phi Delta Kappa, Bloomington.

[17] Glines. D. E. 1978 *Educational Futures III: Change and Reality.* Anvil Press, Millville, MN.

[18] Barnes, R. E. 1972 *Learning Systems for the Future.* Phi Delta Kappa Educational Foundation, Bloomington.

[19] Bowman, J., Kierstead, F., Chris, D., Pulliam, J. 1978 *The Far Side of the Future: Social Problems and Educational Reconstruction.* Education Section of the World Future Society.

[20] Botkin, J., Dimancescu, D., Stata, R., McClellan, J. 1983 *Global Stakes: The Future of High Technology in America.* Ballinger, Cambridge.

[21] Feldman, M. J. 1982 "The Community College Comes of Age." *Educational Record*. Spring: p. 26.

[22] Drucker, P. F. 1981 "The Coming Changes in Our School System." *Wall Street Journal*. 3 March: p. 30.

ABOUT THE AUTHORS

G. EDWARD HARING is Dean of Non-Traditional Education at Elgin Community College, Elgin, Illinois; NCSPOD Vice President for Publications, and a member of its Future Trends Commission. In 1982, he received the coveted John Fry Individual Merit Award from NCSPOD for his outstanding contributions to staff development. Haring formerly taught physics at two-year colleges in Illinois and Indiana as well as at Indiana State University. He is President of the Illinois Community/Junior College Council for Staff, Program and Organizational Development, a member of the American Society for Training and Development, and a child birth educator.

LYNN H. WILLETT is the Vice President for Institutional and Community Development at Elgin Community College, Elgin, Illinois and an adjunct instructor for Southern Illinois University. Currently an Associate Editor for *Community/Junior College Quarterly for Research and Practice*, Willett has published articles in at least seven other academic journals. This former Dean of Community Services has a Ph.D. degree in Higher Education.

5

Diary of the Development of a College/Community Futures Network

G. Edward Haring and Lynn H. Willett

Consider the surrounding community in which you find your organization. The external community is a rich resource of persons from all sectors of the society. The problem which faced the staff at Elgin Community College was how to plug into this loose, formless resource.

The idea of establishing a local futures network was simulated by four sharing ideas at the college. Each of the staff felt a need to share and exchange ideas with a larger, more diverse, group. The formation of a Futures Network from the local community was seen as a challenge. How this group was formed will be detailed in a "collective diary" from the Network originators.

TASK—LAUNCHING THE IDEA OF A FUTURES NETWORK

December 13 — Ed and Lynn discussed their interest in connecting with community members on futuristic ideas. Ed indicated he knew other staff felt the same. Lynn offered lunch if Ed could organize his group.

January 7   — Lunch meeting with Chris, Ed, Tom and Lynn. Agreed to proceed to form group. Everyone would submit community names to Lynn for initial contact. Next meeting January 18 to review progress.

January 18 — Meeting cancelled; no one came!

February 1 — Three members of group met to discuss progress of contacts and to discuss meeting design. Agreed on panel format; *Megatrends* will be discussed. Location at a local pub.

TASK—MARKETING THE MEETING

February   4 — Tom asked Department Dean for money for meeting. Can get $50.

February   9 — Ed requested money from Student Activities. No commitment given.

February 15 — Ed and Tom submitted more community names to Lynn.

February 16 — Lynn wrote letter and mailed to community members. Letter asked for interest and nominations of others who might be interested.

February 18 — Ed, Tom, Chris and Lynn met to complete meeting brochure format, assess community names and status of panel members.

February 19 — Ed and Chris develop meeting process agenda.

February 23 — 400 yellow brochures run off in College copy center. Brochure had registration coupon and requested $1.50 fee which were to be mailed to College Continuing Education office.

March 1   — Ed obtained commitment from College PR staff for a newspaper article announcing meeting.

TASK—FINAL ARRANGEMENTS
FOR FUTURES NETWORK MEETING

March 6   — Brochure mailed to 220 people.

March 11-12   — Lynn designed human resource directory survey to be used at meeting.

March 12   — Newspaper article appeared in local paper at the bottom of the obituary page!

March 13   — Chris checked final details with local pub owner. Indicated we would have fifty people there.

TASK—FIRST MEETING OF THE FUTURES NETWORK

March 14   — Sixty-seven people from all sectors of Fox Valley life attended meeting. Panel discussion was offered on *Megatrends*. Data on participants was collected. Networking opportunities were offered.

TASK—POST MEETING ACTIVITIES

April 11   — Ed, Tom, Chris, Lynn met to review data collected at meeting and to formulate follow-up plans.

April 13   — Ed sent letter to all participants and a copy of the Network's human resource directory.

April 14   — Ed, via telephone, contacted network members who wanted next meeting planning involvement.

April 22   — Planning meeting held with seven members. Topics for fall were selected and resource people identified.

July 31   — Lynn identified several Fox Valley Futures Network members to be linked to College's Long-Range Planning Committee.

The following ingredients for success have been identified. It is felt that the successful formation of the network was the result of using a number of sound social psychological principles in getting started and of using good meeting design.

KEY INGREDIENTS TO THE SUCCESSFUL FORMATION OF A FUTURES NETWORK

1. Utilized existing organization (community college) resources, i.e., mailing, audio-visual, copy center, secretarial.

2. Utilized volunteers for steering committees.

3. Identified and nominated potential community participants via formal and informal approaches.

4. Divided meeting responsibilities among steering committee, thus gaining personal commitment.

5. Presented futures network as a loose, informal, low commitment activity.

The successful launching of the community futures network has been chronicled in this organizers' diary. The network will continue to exist, grow and change as different community members provide leadership and direction. Staff at the organizing community college have begun to establish successful follow-up linkages with various members of the network. The futures network will slowly begin to develop features of cohesion and purpose.

ABOUT THE AUTHOR

GERALDINE A. EVANS is President of
Rochester Community College, Rochester,
Minnesota and the former Director of
Personnel for the Minnesota Community
College System. This former educational
consultant and secondary school counselor
is a school board vice chair and is very
involved in church work, local and state
politics and government and in leading
regional efforts for the Gifted and Talented
in Minnesota. She has authored several
training packages, two monographs, and
several journal articles.

6
Building Excellence In Your College

Geraldine A. Evans

No time in history has produced more criticism of organizational productivity than the present. The national concern over slipping from first in world wealth, innovation, productivity, and prestige to a lesser ranking has caused concern for our work ethic, our management style, and our organizational patterns. No sector of the American life has received more blame for this general decline of our nation in the world standing than education.

During the last ten years, colleges have gone through a period of great stress. After more than a decade of immense growth and unprecedented prestige, we have sunk, during the most recent decade, to an all-time low in national respect. The decline in the number of potential students was followed by a rapid decline in resources and a sharp increase in faculty layoffs. As educators became depressed and uncertain of their stake in the future, they sought the security and power of unions, but have become increasingly disillusioned when this movement did not bring the job satisfaction they hoped for. The move toward unionism somewhat shocked the rest of the nation, and certainly bewildered the managers within education to the point of, at times, rendering them ineffective in directing the destiny of their own institutions.

Used to working with good resources, abundant good will, and collegial staff, college administrators became incapacitated by public criticism, short resources, and disgruntled employees. Education as a profession took the blame for everything from the students' lack of writing and grammar skills to their disrespect for the rules of society; from the high unemployment rate to the decline of the United States in the world economy. We found ourselves quite unable to document and defend ourselves or our achievements.

As educators we were not used to this criticism; it devastated our self-concepts and our feelings of self-worth. We are "people oriented" and thrive on recognition and respect for our job satisfaction. It is unlikely that any group of professionals could have survived without serious scars the societal criticism, sharp curtailment of resources, and personal attacks educators have experienced over the last ten years. However, I believe educators have a higher-than-average need for positive recognition and were particularly disturbed by the turn of events. We lost, or questioned, our mission. We became disoriented, confused, and depressed. We no longer felt ourselves to be a vital force in the building of our great country. Our organizational structures and the people who managed them seemed to be chains around the necks of the employees, and a hindrance in delivering quality instruction.

These years have been rough ones for colleges and, at the present time, few college administrators are pleased with the organizational health of their institutions. As college educators, we have lamented our trials and tribulations long enough. It is now time to realize that the problems we face will not go away with self-pity, explanations, and wishes. As leaders of these colleges, we must assume the responsibility of aggressively moving our organizations on the road to quality again. To realistically change we must, however, have a theoretical base, or a set of rules, for change. Where do we find these, and how do we start?

I believe the book, *In Search of Excellence: Lessons From America's Best Run Companies*, by Thomas Peters and Robert Waterman, Jr., may be one of the best sources of inspiration for the community college administrator today.

McKinsey and Company, a management consulting firm concerned with the present quality of leadership, decided to launch a study of management techniques in an attempt to answer some of the burning questions facing organizations today: "Why do some organizations survive extremely well, while others wallow in mediocrity?" "What is the secret of successful management?" "Does the key really lie in sophisticated equipment, state-of-the-art equipment, and well-planned strategies?"

The authors studied forty-three of what they considered to be the best companies in the nation and found some very surprising results. The authors identified eight attributes that emerged to consistently characterize the best-run companies. They are as follows:

(1) A BIAS FOR ACTION—for getting on with the task of the organization. If a problem exists, well-run companies bring the right people together and expect them to solve the problem as soon as possible. Needs of clients, customers, and employees are addressed and handled speedily.

(2) STAY CLOSE TO THE CUSTOMER. The best companies provide unparalleled, quality service to their customers or clients. They talk to their customers, determine their needs, and assess their satisfaction with the product or service. They change constantly on the basis of the information received to provide a better product or to better serve their clients. Many of the best and innovative companies get their most worthwhile ideas directly from listening to customers.

All of the best-run companies define themselves as service organizations. Whether it was IBM making and selling computers, Minnesota Mining and Manufacturing doing research on a new tape, or McDonald's selling hamburgers, all the excellent companies saw their product as service. Relationships with customers were their primary concern.

(3) HANDS ON—VALUE DRIVEN. Any organization, in order to survive and achieve success, must have a sound set of beliefs on which it premises all of its policies and actions. The basic underlying philosophy of an organization has far more to do with its achievements than do technological and monetary resources, organizational structure, innovation, or

timing.

(4) PRODUCTIVITY THROUGH PEOPLE. Good organizations care about and trust their employees. Their language is people and family oriented. Many of the best companies view themselves as extended families. They value their employees and treat them with respect. The employees enjoy each other and have a good feeling about their work. All employees understand and promote the underlying value of the company. They obtain great satisfaction from being a part of the process of accomplishing the mission.

(5) AUTONOMY AND ENTREPRENEURSHIP. The best companies foster leaders and innovators throughout the organization. They allow people to experiment and to make mistakes without serious consequences. They do not hold employees on too short a rein. They encourage "fired-up champions" to carry out projects rather than confining them to the layers of the bureaucracy. These innovators may be at any level of the organization. No matter how large the company, great companies all "act small."

(6) STICK TO THE KNITTING. Good organizations stay very close to their central mission. Such organizations never get into projects or enterprises that they do not really know how to run. They do not go on sojourns where their expertise does not follow.

(7) SIMULTANEOUS LOOSE-TIGHT PROPERTIES. Good organizations are rigidly controlled on the basic principles of operation. However, they control *only* the essentials. and allow great autonomy in how the work is accomplished. A few shared values and beliefs provide the framework for innovation and freedom. Discipline provides the framework for freedom of thought and action.

(8) SIMPLE FORM—LEAN STAFF. Making an organization work has everything to do with making the operation simple and easily understandable to those who make things happen. That really means keeping out the many layers of bureaucracy that can stifle communication.

These eight attributes are not really surprising. The rules are so logical and sensible! Somehow we have let ourselves believe management must be more complicated and "scientific" than it really is. We have all known how important it is to use student input in planning and evaluating our activities, but some of our ineffectiveness now, I am sure, comes from getting too many layers of administration between the student and the president. The authors seem to be telling us to get back to the simple, commonsense basics of caring about people.

First, we need to redefine and clearly state our reason for existence. We need to be sure we really know what we are striving for. This reason for existence must, obviously, be centered around service to students. This mission must be communicated to all of our employees in such a way as to be the central driving force of the organization. If all employees—administrators, faculty, and support staff— understand this underlying value, there should be little question or concern regarding directions, priorities, and allocation of resources. Such an underlying, well-known, and pervasive value should resolve many of the internal struggles that can often occur if conflicting value directions are present within the staff.

Along with this underlying value, the college should set down a very few specific and well-known principles of action. Beyond these, the rules and policies should be kept to a minimum, and employees should be trusted to do their very best in their own creative and innovative way to achieve the college mission.

Several of the basic principles direct our attention toward simplifying the organization and building close relationships with the people who deliver our service. The book makes it clear that layers of bureaucracy hinder our ability to allow the employees to be innovative and creative. Productivity through people is also hindered if our colleges become encumbered with too many levels of authority. Such stratifying hampers our ability to act quickly and decisively when a problem occurs. This inability to act in a timely fashion affects morale and discourages creativeness in employees.

And lastly, the advice of the authors in their "stick to the knitting" principle is vital. Almost every college has been guilty of going off on some tangential "good cause," and found the venture a failure. The authors tell us that we are in trouble when we spread ourselves too thin or go into enterprises where we lack expertise. Channeled focus and narrow goals are more easily managed, and more clearly understood.

In summary, I believe the message of *In Search of Excellence* to the community college administrator today, is quite straightforward. Find and clearly state your purpose. Be sure to define yourself as a *service* agency. Stay close to the needs and desires of the student body and develop ways of listening to your students. Let all of your staff know the central purpose for the college's existence so it is a driving force in each employee's day. Keep a few simple, easily communicated rules, which all are expected to follow, but do not hamper action by too many rules. Keep your organizational plan simple, so as to facilitate good communication. Respect and trust your employees to do a good job for you; free your employees to carry-out the mission of your college in their own creative and innovative way. This is how I believe you will build excellence in your college today.

ABOUT THE AUTHORS

DAVID R. PIERCE is the Executive Director of the Illinois Community College Board
and a former community college president
as well as an administrator and faculty
member at colleges in Iowa, Illinois, and
California. He has a Ph.D. degree in Mathematics Education, is an evaluator/consultant
for the North Central Association of Colleges and Schools and a member of AACJC's
Commission on Governmental Affairs. In
Illinois, Pierce is a member of the Illinois
Job Training Coordinating Council and the
Governor's Task Force on Private Sector
Initiatives.

ANN KIEFFER BRAGG is Director of
Program Planning for the Illinois Community College Board and the holder of a
D. Ed. degree in Higher Education. She is
the former Director of the Office of Educational Relations and Special Assistant to
the Senior Vice President for Administration
at Penn State University. Bragg also served as
Assistant Dean of Women at St. Olaf College
in Northfield, Minnesota.

7

The Community College Challenge for the Future: A State Agency Viewpoint

David R. Pierce and Ann Kieffer Bragg

A change in state policy toward education during the past few years has profoundly altered the role of the community colleges and the state-level agency for community colleges. From being a nearly ignored—though necessary—state responsibility, community colleges have suddenly become the crucial member of the state's economic development team.

In this chapter, we will review briefly the primary forces behind this change and discuss the challenges they present for the future to community colleges and to state-level agencies for community colleges.

ENVIRONMENTAL FORCES

Three major trends, each laden with contradictions and permutations, are now merging to cause a disjuncture in American life. The first, an economic trend, was viewed a few years ago as simply another pendulum swing from inflation to recession. This trend is now recognized for what it is: the beginning of a new economic age. Since 1972, with the birth of the silicon chip, the information-based economy took off, and the industrial-based economy continued its decline. By 1982, only 13 percent of the U.S. labor force were employed in manufacturing, while 60 percent were employed in some phase of the creation, analysis, or dissemination of information.[1]

By 1990, microprocessors will be everywhere. With continuing price declines and further technological advances, portable and transportable microcomputers have already captured more than 50 percent of the computer market.[2] In the office, computers and word processors are now nearly as common as typewriters. In industry, robots are taking over the routine and dangerous jobs, while providing increased quality control. The use of robots quadrupled between 1979 and 1981,[3] and is expected to continue to double every three years.[4] Theoretically, at least, 65 to 75 percent of the factory workforce will be replaced by automation.[5] What was "chronic" unemployment has become "structural" unemployment as persons losing jobs to the recession, to plant closings, and to automation cannot enter the new job market without retraining. Retraining, indeed, will be needed every ten years.[6]

Data processing, telecommunications, laser and fiber optics, robotics, and pharmaceuticals and genetic engineering—the high technology industries—rely heavily on education in selecting a location. An educated workforce and continuing educational and cultural amenities for their employees, instead of transportation, water, and energy, are prime requirements. Corporations that cannot find appropriate training programs start their own. Wang, IBM, and "Hamburger U" are but examples of the growing number of corporately owned educational institutions with degree-granting authority.

In a decade when "computer literacy" and "reasoning," as the fourth "R," are being touted as skills required of all high school graduates, the gulf between the educated "haves" and the under-educated "have nots" is widening. Approximately 23 million American adults are functionally illiterate, and what is more discouraging, a number of states—e.g., California, Ohio, and Wisconsin—are reporting dramatic increases in the number of high school dropouts.[7]

The second trend is the changing demographics of the U.S. population. By 1990, the "bulge" of the post-war baby boom will swell the ranks of the 24-44 age cohort by 14 million, and the over-65 age group will increase by five million. The high school and college-age cohort, on the other hand, will decline by seven million by 1990.[8] This age shift will result in fewer students entering college directly from high school, fewer young people entering the labor market, and a "greying" of the workforce, including the faculties and staffs of colleges and universities.

The traditional American family of Dad, the breadwinner, and Mom at home with their two children is no longer the norm. By 1985, fully 60 percent of American households will include only one or two persons. More and more Americans are now living alone—before marriage, between marriages, and after the death of a spouse, and increasing numbers of women are entering the labor force. In 1982, more than half of women 16 years and older were in the labor force. By 1990, 75 percent of the 25-54 year old women will be employed outside the home.[9] There is a growing number of not just "two-job," but "dual-career," households.

The third trend is a dramatic change in attitude of the American people. Americans are no longer optimistic about the future of the country or themselves. In a recent issue of *Forbes*,[10] Thomas Murphy described a conversation with the Fairfield University sociologist, Arthur Anderson, who indicated that "Surveys in the past always found us the most optimistic people in the world. Now, one survey I saw places us 17th in the Free World." Murphy concluded, "So Anderson sees a pessimistic America, cherishing small luxuries because the big ones are out of reach." For the first time, Americans do not see themselves exceeding their parents' achievements, as the lifetime earnings differential between high school and college graduates narrows and the surplus of doctoral-degree holders mounts.

Americans have come to distrust big government and big business as ineffective and inefficient in solving today's problems. Yet the reaction is not the social protest of the late 1960s, but rather one of increasing reliance on self. The rise of do-it-yourself home building and repair, growing one's own food, buying cooperatives, self-care health practices, and urban neighborhood associations all reflect this growing trend.[11] Participatory democracy in neighborhood associations and city/township government has led to a greater demand for participatory democracy in the workplace. Management teams and quality circles are becoming a common means of providing input into decision making by the persons who must implement the decisions.

The emphasis in buying habits is shifting toward the natural, toward high quality and durability, and toward conservation, with conspicious consumption on the decline. This demand for quality extends to education. Recent months have brought a flurry of reports—The National Commission on Excellence in Education's report "A Nation at Risk;" the Education Commission of the States' Task Force on Education for Economic Growth report "Action for Excellence;" The National Commission on Higher Education Issues' report "To Strengthen Quality in Higher Education;" and the Carnegie Foundation for the Advancement of Teaching's "High School: A Report on Secondary Education in America" and the National Science Board's Commission on Precollege Education in Mathematics, Science, and Technology report "Educating Americans for the 21st Century." These reports are receiving much play in the press and are likely to engender controversy. Although the outsome of these demands for quality are as yet uncertain nationwide, we will all likely be called upon to defend publicly what we are doing and why.

In sum, the three trends of structural unemployment and high technology, the changing demographics of the population, and a change in public attitudes will buffet the community colleges unless we anticipate the demands and rise to the challenge.

THE CHALLENGE FOR COMMUNITY COLLEGES

The high technology/information revolution presents mixed signals to community colleges. On the one hand, new high technology industries and the use of high technology in the office suggest a need for improved skills in electronics and "computer talk." On the other, however, the greatest absolute number of new jobs created by 1990 likely will be in "low technology"—janitors, nurses aides, clerks, cashiers, and waiters/waitresses.[12] In the past, the introduction of

new technologies has reduced, rather than increased, the level of skill necessary as each job was broken down into smaller, more routinized segments. Do we as community colleges need to provide more basic skills and general education to help people cope with rapid changes or do we need to provide increasingly specialized training? It is our sense that both are required—and now!

The community colleges are recognized as the institutions most able to adjust rapidly to changing employment demand and as the institutions that already train a large share of today's technicians, operators, installers, and repairers. The challenge will be to live up to and amplify this reputation. Community colleges must prepare now to train the computer, world processor, computer-aided design/computer-aided manufacturing (CAD/CAM), robot, telecommunication, and medical equipment technicians, operators, installers, and repairers of the future. No community college, for example, should offer secretarial science programs without word processing, or drafting programs without CAD training. We must also make provisions for our prior graduates to learn these new, required skills. Computer literacy will need to be a community college graduation requirement—at least until it becomes a high school graduation requirement.

The ability of any community college to mount high technology programs will depend on the local job market for the program's completers and on the availability of resources for equipment, faculty, and facilities. We will need to be creative in meeting these resource needs, since resources are unlikely to increase greatly from present sources—local, state, and federal taxes and tuition. One new source of funding with considerable promise is the federal Job Training Partnership Act (JTPA). In Illinois, twelve community colleges have already been designated Dislocated Workers Training Centers under Title III to provide training and services to people who have lost their jobs due to plant closings, mass layoffs, and changes in technology, and several community colleges have been selected to administer their service delivery areas (SDAs). It will be up to us to make this new Act work.

An often overlooked and increasingly imperative funding

source is the internal reallocation of existing resources. Any reallocation of resources must be firmly tied to a thorough review of existing programs and services and a concomitant commitment to phase out low-quality, low-need, and obsolete programs. Such a commitment will depend on a shared vision of the future of the college by all of our constituents.

The formation of partnerships and other cooperative arrangements with business and industry and among community colleges can expand both the labor market and the resources available for the new program. Cooperation with local industry, for example, can provide an immediate employment outlet for program graduates, a sharing of expensive equipment, and a pooling of expertise for faculty and curriculum development. With the assistance of expert advisory committees, as well as the aggressive and insightful leadership of the colleges' staffs, several Illinois community colleges have received donations, or partial donations, of such high technology equipment as CAD/CAM, numerical control machines, and industrial and training robots and of complex software packages in order to develop and implement new state-of-the-art programs in these areas. Each college also set aside the funds necessary to send faculty and staff members to training programs, industrial exhibitions, and conferences and on site visits around the country in order to gain the required expertise to train students in the role and use of the new technology and to develop appropriate curricula.

Cooperation with neighboring institutions also can expand the labor market area and distribute the costs of equipment and costs for the development of faculty and curriculum over a broader base. Similar to the public school concept of "magnet schools," North Carolina has designated each of its technical institutes to become the provider of a different high technology program. In Illinois, voluntary inter-district cooperative agreements, in which each college admits students from the other district to those programs not offered by the other district, are encouraged. In this way, a critical mass of students is assured the receiving district, and the sending district can provide access to programs which the district itself cannot justify offering.

In the rush to develop high technology programs, however, we cannot ignore what may well be our biggest challenge—the need to teach basic skills to the 23 million adults
who cannot read, write, compute, or "reason." By whatever
rubric we choose, whether it be remedial, developmental,
compensatory, or adult education, our role in providing
basic skill training must continue to increase. Competency-
testing, open entry/open exit, computer-aided instruction,
storefront extension, TV courses, volunteer and paid student
tutors, and effective relationships with community agencies
who can identify individuals needing skills must all be explored, mobilized, and melded into a program to meet this
critical need.

To be able to make the programmatic changes required in
the future, each college's organizational structure must be
flexible—flexible enough to capitalize on new opportunities
quickly. Rigidity in reporting lines and artificial barriers
created by structure or policy will need to be removed or
ameliorated. The administrative separation of transfer and
occupational programs, for example, may limit understanding
of the need for general education in occupational programs
and the need for career exploration experiences in transfer
programs. The assignment of basic skill training to a continuing education division or school may likewise prevent
prospective degree- or certificate-seeking students from ob-
taining the assistance they need to succeed in their chosen
program. Colleges will need a research and planning capability but not necessarily an office of research and planning.
Community colleges that have not already done so need to
develop streamlined processes for institutional planning and
priority setting, for the approval of new curricula and the
review of existing programs and services, and for faculty and
staff development, updating, and retraining. Team management and faculty and staff participation in these processes
will be essential to building consensus on the future directions of the college.

The "greying of America" will present another challenge
for faculty and staff development. The community college
full-time faculty is aging as decreasing turnover, a slowing of
institutional growth, and the tenuring-in phenomena reach
their peaks. Orientation, professional development, and

participation of part-time faculty members, particularly, will be crucial if part-timers are to continue to provide a growing share of community college instruction. The college's vision will be sabotaged if part-timers do not share that vision. Care must be taken in developing collective bargaining agreements to protect class schedule flexibility and the implementation of new priorities and directions. Just as we will be called upon to retrain displaced workers in industry, we also will need to provide opportunities for our faculty and staff members to retrain and upgrade their skills in this information age.

The state agency for community colleges also must change. The state agency for community colleges must become the broker among the other state agencies involved in education and jobs, as well as among the community colleges. The agency must take on greater information-processing tasks: it must compile, analyze, and disseminate information on labor markets, new curricula, new sources of funding, and the quality of the community college product—our graduates. The state agency also will need to develop greater research and planning capabilities, not as a separate unit in the agency, but as a continuous part of every function over which it has authority. The Illinois Community College Board staff, for example, has recently reorganized, disbanding the separate research division, and assigning a full-time researcher to the remaining program and operations/fiscal divisions in order to highlight and incorporate planning and research into each division's ongoing, daily responsibilities. Our computerized managment information system is now becoming one of the tools for planning, rather than the end product.

With the advent of high technology, regional and state-wide planning will need to become the norm, and state agencies too will need to establish priorities in the kinds of programs they approve and fund. If it does not already do so, the state agency must recognize the legitimacy of basic skills instruction as an important community college function. If it has program-approval authority, the state agency must shorten the length of time it takes to approve a new program while at the same time strengthening the tie between program approval and program need at the state, regional, and local levels. In addition, the state agency must examine the need for "sunset" provisions on program approval so that programs without graduates or for which there is no longer an employment need can be terminated. The Illinois Community College Board, for example, is re-examining its policies in order to streamline approval processes and reduce paperwork burdens so that we can shift our agency resources to help colleges meet the challenges ahead. We in state agencies need to contribute to the solution or we will become part of the problem.

The future for community colleges, without question, can be very bright. The major limitation will be ourselves—whether we have the vision, flexibility, spirit, and zeal to rise to meet it. There has never been a time when there has been a greater demand for education. The only question is whether we, as educational leaders, are up to the challenge.

REFERENCES

[1] Naisbitt, J. 1982 *Megatrends: Ten New Directions Transforming Our Lives.* Warner Books, New York:14.

[2] Geller, I. 1983 "Business Outlook—Portable Computers: A Hot Market." *High Technology.* 3(9):52.

[3] Levitan, S. A., Johnson, C. M. 1982 "The Future of Work: Does it Belong to Us or to the Robots?" *Monthly Labor Review.* September: 11.

[4] Kiplinger, A. 1982 *The Kiplinger Washington Letter.* 59(52):3.

[5] Levitan, S. A., Johnson, C. M. 1982 "The Future of Work: Does it Belong to Us or to the Robots?" *Monthly Labor Review.* September: 11.

[6] Cetron, M. 1983 "Career Planning for 2000 A.D." *Success.* September: 25.

[7] Naisbitt, J. 1982 *Megatrends: Ten New Directions Transforming Our Lives.* Warner Books, New York: 32.

[8] Kiplinger, A. 1982 *The Kiplinger Washington Letter.* 59(52):1.

[9] Kiplinger, A. 1982 *The Kiplinger Washington Letter.* 59(52):2.

[10] Murphy, T. 1983 "Giving up on the American Dream." *Forbes.* 29 August: 166.

[11] Naisbitt, J. 1982 *Megatrends: Ten New Directions Transforming Our Lives.* Warner Books, New York: 131-157.

[12] Levin, H. M., Rumberger, R. W. 1983 *Educational Implications of High Technology.* Institute for Research on Educational Finance and Governance, Stanford University, Stanford.

ABOUT THE AUTHOR

DON C. GARRISON is President of Tri-County Technical College, Pendleton, South Carolina, President of the Aerospace Education Foundation and a member of the Board of Trustees of the American Council on Education and the ACCTion Coordinating Board. He is also co-chair of the AACJC/ACCT "Putting America Back to Work" Task Force and a member of the Board of Directors of Community colleges for International Development. Formerly, Garrison was a member of the AACJC Board of Directors, a member of the Eric Advisory Council for Community/Junior Colleges, and chair of the AACJC Presidents Academy.

8
Putting America Back to Work:
Post-Industrial Society, Community Colleges, the Future, and Implications for SPOD

By Don C. Garrison

Most people would agree today that America is well on the way to lowering the highest national unemployment rate our country has experienced since World War II. It is also safe to advance a wide variety of reasons for this major economic dilemma, and why this same dilemma is now on the demise. There is, however, one basic fact that relates to the future economic health and global competitive posture of our nation in commerce and trade; that is, the accelerating development of the post-industrial technological society.

John Naisbitt's *Megatrends*, and other best-selling publications which relate to this subject, clearly illustrate that fundamental restructuring and dramatic changes with major trends and directions are now transforming our lives and evolving a new world. A fundamental fact often obscured by these great changes is that people have to have a job and have to be engaged in meaningful, productive work. Eleven- and twelve-percent national unemployment rates are, by all standards, unaffordable by the nation and socially unacceptable. Some futurists, economists and organizations projected well in advance of our recent national economic tailspin that the tailspin was coming and they postulated varied reasons.

The American Association of Community and Junior Colleges through its board of directors, established a task force in late 1981 upon recommendation of its newly-elected president, Dale Parnell, to establish a task force to lead a major association initiative to address these concerns.

The roots for this AACJC continuing thrust lie in one of its many affiliate councils, the Council for Occupational Education. The COE at its 1981 annual fall seminar adopted a resolution which recognized the absence of a national human resource development policy as contrasted to other leading industrialized nations. The resolution also called for the AACJC to provide leadership in bringing about, with strong corporate involvement and support, presidential initiative and congressional action to develop a national human resource development policy for the United States.

Following through on the AACJC's board action, Dale Parnell established a task force, later chaired by this writer, to initiate a project which continues presently and operates under the heading of a concept paper issued by the AACJC. This concept paper, presented at the AACJC annual convention in March of 1982, is entitled "Putting America Back to Work." This paper proposes a "moon shot" commitment to foster job development and training relevant to economic development. The paper also states clearly that the nation's 1,234 community and technical colleges residing in practically every congressional district represent a major national resource for any effort to retrain America's workforce.

The great capital investments at these colleges are providing, or can provide, high-quality, modestly priced, custom-designed training programs for American business and industry. As a result of the first year of work of the task force, the W. K. Kellogg Foundation funded, in part, continuation of this vital AACJC initiative.

During 1983, the American Association of Community College Trustees joined this initiative as a partner of the AACJC, and a new joint task force was appointed. Other foundation support has been achieved to continue into 1984 this all-important project. It is not necessary for me to delve into the mission, growth, development, and record of service to community, state and nation of the community and technical colleges in America. What our colleges can do, and do, is well documented.

It is important to recognize, however, that a major trend in these colleges is underway on a college-to-college, region-to-region and state-to-state basis. This trend can be attributed partially to the work of the task force and its parent associations of the "Putting America Back to Work" project. The trend is exemplified by three facts. They are:

1. Beginning a few years ago and for the first time ever, more than 50 percent of the freshmen enrolled in higher education institutions in America were enrolled in community and technical colleges and, of these, over 50 percent were enrolled in occupation-specific programs.

2. Colleges, in response to community (local business and industry) needs, continue to invest heavily in new high-tech programs and equipment being introduced almost daily by the technological revolution.

3. Colleges have recognized that they can be key elements in local, regional and state economic development/growth formulas and, therefore, are stimulating and leading initiatives for the creation of such formulas and are insuring that they are included in such formulas. An example is the writer's own college and the state system of which the college is a part.

Time and space do not permit elaboration on the many resultant forces being generated by the post-industrial, technological society and the rapidly expanding world economy in our respective communities, our states, and our nation. Suffice it to point out, however, that a prime contributing factor to our recent record unemployment rate is the loss of jobs to other countries which have embraced American-generated knowledge and technology in manufacturing output and productivity growth and, therefore, have captured large portions of what used to be our American share of world markets.

Third world developing countries compete in the world market-place with immeasurably cheap, all-but-slave-wage labor and now control a commanding position formerly occupied by the United States. A failure on our part as a nation over the past decade-plus to recognize and respond to these forces contributes to a great degree to the loss of our share of world markets in auto sales, wide-body jet aircraft sales, soybean and steel markets and consumer electronics. This loss occurred at a time when world-wide trade grew from $150-billion to $1.5-trillion.

One can certainly postulate that, if our nation had maintained to the present its share of the world market that it commanded during the 60s and had achieved at the same time a comparable amount of the growth of world trade, the economic health and current employment rate would be more positive today.

Automation in the work place—the application of new, advanced, cutting-edge, high-technology equipment, best exemplified by robotics, microelectronics, computers, and word processors—will increase worker productivity and enable our country to win the global economic war that we are now losing. By the same token, automation will dislocate workers, eliminate jobs, create new and different jobs, force the creation of the highest-educated worker ever and, *most critical of all to community and technical college educators, generate many opportunities for valuable and, in many cases, necessary community services.*

One of these services falls in the area of retraining dislocated workers. Many colleges, not nearly enough, are utilizing available C.E.T.A. (Comprehensive Education Training Act) and the new (October 1, 1983) J.T.P.A. (Job Training Partnership Act) resources as a means of financing strong, highly responsive programs to retrain dislocated workers. Use of regular college funding, however, should be considered if we are unable to acquire federal J.T.P.A. funds to respond to this community need.

Retraining of workers who remain at work and whose jobs have changed due to new high-tech equipment represents another major avenue of college service to community needs. In some states, funds for retraining programs demand a priority as high as the funding of the established degree and certificate programs.

Job creation resulting from economic growth and new, risk-capital investment is the third and most critical avenue of service. College management policies, procedures and philosophy, combined with similar faculty flexibility and "can do" attitudes, are essential to successful college service to the community and its people by fostering job security and growth. The college must acknowledge that the highest job growth over the next decade will be in service industries, meaning that the college will need to develop and implement programs for service industries. Local and national companies, meanwhile, spend billions of dollars annually on internal training programs that local colleges could conduct, thereby increasing the productivity and efficiency of these companies while reducing their operating costs.

National chains of private vocational schools flourish today because they maximize the training market. Many, in fact, are teaching high-tech subjects and their enrollment and profits are growing. Obviously, they receive no direct public financial support but still turn a profit. David Fottlieb, writing in the October, 1983, *High Technology*, predicts that "a large and growing business will emerge in training for the new skills that will be needed in the coming decade."

The community/technical college, with its mandate, its purpose of serving community, its community base, its unique characteristics as truly American in origin, its flexibility, its "people's college" concept, its student-learning-teaching centered nature and its reason for being, is without question one of the greatest resources of the community, the state and the nation. This resource should be maximized as our nation responds to the global war in the competition for our accustomed share of world markets. By reclaiming our share of the market, we will create jobs and improve job security for more Americans than would otherwise prevail. If these colleges, of which we are all a part, do their job then, indeed, the above facts must be recognized and a college service response which is timely, successful and which fully accomplishes the objective is necessary.

This, I believe, is where SPOD is so vital to each community/technical college. I believe the greatest challenge faced by the chief executive officer of any given community/technical college is that of *maximizing all of the resources available to the college.* These resources are obviously varied and many. Among the more important of these resources are the dollars which make possible the most critical of all of the college's resources, its full-time and part-time faculty and staff. Of course, dollars also are necessary to purchase equipment, supplies and facilities. Advisory committee members, elected officials who appropriate dollars, lay people in the community who support the college financially through its foundation, are another valuable resource.

The single greatest resource available to the college, however, is its people—its faculty and staff. Maximizing this most precious of all resources of the college is essential if, indeed, the dollars (majority) which are invested in making this college resource available are to be maximized. Industry and business recognize this premier point as evidenced by the $50-billion-plus they invest in education and training activities annually for their employees. Colleges which fail to respond in a similar fashion fail to protect their investment in this invaluable college resource. Colleges which fail to invest in their faculty, staff and program development also fail because they lower their ability to provide the quality, relevant and, therefore, cutting-edge education and training required by todays high-tech society. This high-tech society resides at the grass-roots community served by your college. This factor has never been more critical than today because of the enrollment patterns and trends of growing occupational programs.

High-tech program initiatives represent one of the greatest challenges faced by community/technical colleges today. A resultant challenge is that of keeping faculty and staff working at a knowledge edge that, indeed, is at best near the "cutting edge" or at least in a "fast follow" mode. The same, of course, can be said for program and organizational development. Programs which fail to keep up-to-date and in touch with the times cannot be tolerated if resources are to be maximized. Along with other colleges across the country, Tri-County Technical College has terminated programs because they were no longer relevant. If programs are not maintained at a level consistent with the technology as incorporated in the job structure in the community they are not relevant. If not relevant, they do not and cannot serve the community. They are then obsolete and must be closed just as a business or industrial manufacturing establishment must close its doors and board its windows when it is unable to be productive and competitive.

Organizational development is, of all of the elements of

SPOD, most critical. This writer believes that this is the very area where our nation's business and industries permitted Japan, West Germany and other industrial nations to slip up on us and take away our command of the world trade market. These organizations failed to stay in touch with what was going on around them, in the nation and in the world. They failed to recognize the competition and permitted vacuums to be created and then others filled the vacuums. They, in turn, were forced to close their doors, file for bankruptcy and send the workers home with no jobs. The workers' next stop was today's long unemployment lines.

Organizations must stay in touch with the times by using strategic planning, emerging viable management techniques, and improved cost-benefit programs and initiatives. In essence, each unit, each person of every unit of the organization, is critical in maximizing every resource available to the college. Every dollar must generate the biggest possible "bang." From housekeeping to energy management, from resource ($s) development to community and college research and development, all must practice what we know to be true. We know that the post-industrial technological society of today is a life-long learning society. To be productive—to be a worthy, *contributing* member of the college family—for the community, our society and nation, we must all recognize that when we stop growing we begin to die, then rot and decay and become less than our capability. So it is with SPOD.

"SPODers" best recognize the all-important essence of the green, growing, developing, wonderful American entity, the community-technical college. "SPODers" must continue to be aggressive and relentless in making their vital mission a success. The future of the American community/technical college, to a major degree, depends on just how successful SPOD is in the remaining years of the present decade.

ABOUT THE AUTHOR

DEL A. SHEPARD is Manager of the
Human Resources Department of Des
Moines Area Community College,
Ankeny, Iowa, and holds a Ph.D.
degree in Higher Education Administration. This former marketing and
industrial management instructor
has taught at community colleges
and has taught organizational development and team building at Iowa
State University and the University
of Northern Iowa. A member of
NCSPOD, Shepard was co-presenter
of the Organizational Development
track at the NCSPOD Annual Midwest
Skills Building Conference and has
designed and implemented a successful
comprehensive organizational development program and pervasive institutional restructuring plan for a community college of over 350 full-time
faculty and staff and over 1,150 part-
time instructors. He is also a trained
and certified Quality Circles facilitator.

9

Organizational Development & the Future: Designing Organizational Structures To Match the Changing Mission of the Community College

Del A. Shepard

AN HISTORICAL PERSPECTIVE

Higher education today is undergoing a transformation, particularly at the community college level. The late 1960s and early 1970s saw an increase in enrollments, expansion of building projects, development of new programs and course offerings and the addition of new staff at record rates. Along with this growth in the size of the community college came increased levels of funding to support new initiatives in the field of vocational-technical education. Job training for the high school graduate was emphasized as a high priority and many non-job related courses were not included in the curriculum of many of these training programs.

Because the universities and four year colleges were not as adaptable to changing their programming quickly enough to meet the changing needs of the younger work force, the community colleges continued to grow with great success. Special sources of funding were provided by both state and federal agencies to encourage the further development of programming designed to train and to retrain workers in vocational-technical career fields.

There were more clearly defined divisional lines drawn

within the majority of the community colleges in the types of programs being offered. The more traditional liberal arts courses being offered were delivered by general education or arts and sciences divisions. Generally, students who sought to transfer to a senior institution upon the completion of their studies at the two-year college took classes and received an associate of arts or science degree. The emphasis for the transfer students was their success in getting all the necessary courses taken and being accepted by a senior institution.

For some universities, it was the first time in their history that they found a form of competition not experienced before. The acceptance of students from community colleges was reaching a scale larger than ever before, and many of the academic notions of the four-year schools were being challenged by the two-year schools. Articulation agreements were difficult to work out initially, but eventually many of the senior institutions came to realize that community colleges were serving a market that four-year schools would not have reached—the students that originally had not planned to attend college. Because of successful experiences at the community colleges, the students found an easier adjustment to the four-year institutions.

The vocational-technical or career education students, on the other hand, found programming that was designed more for entry-level occupations in a specific field of study. The programs were designed with very specific goals in mind—to train workers to fill jobs available in the local community or the surrounding geographic area. Several occupational fields flucuated in their demands which caused the increase or decrease of classes required to meet the demands of business and industry. In the earlier years, new programs were designed, staff hired, students recruited and classes started even before adequate equipment and facilities were available. Students overlooked the problems because they were a part of an exciting new venture in education. The staff saw their institutions growing and many shortcomings were excused, because everone was concentrating on handling the growth.

A SYSTEM OF DIVISIONS

The community colleges of today are designed with a

system of divisions which are structurally sound for an institution that grew so rapidly. This structure, however, is posing a threat to the future viability of these same institutions with regard to their ability to deliver services to a client with changing needs. There is a strong need for the organizational structure of community colleges to change if they are to maintain current levels of effectiveness and efficiency in terms of delivery of educational services to the community they serve.

As a result of the system of divisions that has been allowed to develop over the years, there are several problems that arise, not the least of which is duplication of services within the institutions. Examples include duplicated and decentralized recordkeeping systems, dual supervision of staff members, duplicate delivery of like services, excessive levels of administrative staff, and multiple and uncoordinated contacts with clients in business and industry.

Current structural systems should be analyzed in terms of their contribution to the mission of the institution. Many times, the original purposes established for the college are still in place; however, the question must be asked if the institution has continued to refine and update its mission statement. An even more important consideration would be whether the institution has identified goals, objectives and action plans to assist the staff of the college in reaching the mission. The institution must follow through with the process of evaluating the end results against the originally stated objectives.

ORGANIZATIONAL DESIGN

Similar to the design of a complex building, the organizational design of an institution has many facets to be considered. It is interesting to contrast the complexity of design and construction of the physical plant of many community colleges with the resources that are expended on the faculty and staff of the institution.

It may be a natural tendency to spend more time and money on the more concrete, material facilities of an institution than on its people. After all, buildings are not expected to design, construct and improve themselves. They must be carefully maintained if they are to last as long as planned and to deliver the level of service expected from the large investment of capital expenditures.

On the other hand, what investments should be made in the design and improvement of the human resources utilized within the institution? Who are the designers of the institution's organizational structure and what experiences do they have that enable them to carry out their task? If the community colleges are to change, there must be a realization that there is a need for the change. Many times, those that are the closest to the situation are the ones that have the most difficulty in identifying the problems and even more difficulty in designing solutions to those problems.

Just as there are no blueprints that are perfect for the construction of a building, there are no perfect solutions to the challenges of designing an organizational structure that will meet the needs of the institution. There are, however, some very serious considerations to be made in addressing the issue of organizational design and development.

One must ask the following questions when considering the current organizational design of an institution:

1. Does the mission of the college match the structural make-up of the institution?

2. If the mission of the organization has changed, has the structural design changed as well?

3. Does the current structure of the organization serve to frustrate the mission or to facilitate the effective operation of the institution?

4. Does the structure of the institution prevent its members from achieving its mission?

A concern that should be given attention, centers around the identification of a structural design which can make effective use of the existing facilities, equipment and more importantly, the people within the organization. A continual emphasis should be placed on the revitalization of existing members of the organization, rather than the replacement of the valuable resources with less experienced staff. The transition from the past to the present, and then to plan for the future,

takes experience and understanding and can be more effectively accomplished by making use of the college's staff.

This is not to say that there is no need to bring into the
institution fresh ideas and younger blood, quite the contrary.
It takes a blending of ideas, experiences and perspectives to
make such a dramatic change in an institution that has been
in existence for even as short a period of time as 15 to 20
years. The longer the college has been established, the more
time will be required to affect changes in the design and
structure.

Organizational design is the picture of the institution at a
point in time. No organization remains static. Community
colleges are noted for their ability to realize a need for change,
as well as their ability to make changes. However, change for
the sake of change is not the answer to an organizational
design problem.

The organization must be assessed from the standpoint of
its stated mission. From this point forward, the structural
make-up of the institution must be molded to fit the direction of the future. For example, if an institution has always
served high school graduates who are attending college within
one to two years after leaving the secondary system, then
recruitment efforts will be placed on reaching those students.
If however, there is a decline in the number of high school
graduates, as there is in many areas of the country, and there
is an increase in the number of non-traditional students, then
the emphasis should be shifted to the recruitment of students
who have been out of high school for some time and are
more than likely working in full-time occupations. This
sounds like a minor change for the institution at first glance;
but, when more than recruitment is considered, the challenge
becomes much more complex.

Issues such as the delivery of counseling services, development of student government activities, learning resource
development, scheduling of classes for both day and evening
students, weekend classes, etc., all have an impact on the
institution. When a focus is made on the students being served
and their needs, it becomes obvious that a great deal is at
stake when any organizational design changes are anticipated.

IDENTIFYING CHANGE AGENTS

Each organization has within itself members who seek to make innovative changes and are willing to take the risks involved in stepping forward to assist with such changes. Some influence can be made from outside change agents to lend assistance in the form of design change techniques. However, the actual change must come from within the institution and by the members of the organization if the changes are to be at all effective.

Particular attention should be given to the selection of change agents from various levels of the organization. A top-down approach may tend to create resistance to the change and a lack of trust as to what is really going to happen to the members of the organization in the transition period. By bringing into focus those people that are noted for affecting change, the leadership of the institution can make more effective use of these talents and at the same time get the necessary involvement of the people being affected by the changes.

A balance should be maintained, however, between the younger employees and the more experienced staff, the professional and classified staff, the idea generators and the people who can carry out the designed tasks and, most of all, those that are for and those that may be against making changes in the structure of the organization. The attention to this detail can pay off with big dividends in the future as the plans are being set into place.

OD AND STAFF DEVELOPMENT

Organizational design and development can be accomplished in a very effective manner by bringing into play the element of staff development. As mentioned earlier, an emphasis should be placed upon the utilization of existing human resources within the organization. To do this may well require that some individuals change their roles within the institution. This change can be a meaningful experience if handled properly. It will, however, take adequate training on the job as well as in the classroom in some instances. This may also require that some individuals make rather major changes in their careers, to remain a member of the organization. The responsibility rests with the top management of the college to provide the necessary tools to allow for a smooth transition of these individuals from assignments with which they are familiar to assignments that are new and unknown. These changes can be exciting and serve as a means of revitalization for those who have become static in their careers.

Support and leadership for any changes in the structure of the institution must come from the top-level management. A good example of willingness to make and accept changes must be evidenced by members of the top management team of the organization. Along with this support must come an adequate amount of time and understanding to allow for the changes to become a reality.

CHANGING MISSION

Community colleges must remain the vital, community-based institutions that they are today, and yet be willing to meet the challenges of the future. Just as people change, so have their demands for education. Today's society is seeking answers to questions that did not exist just a few decades ago. Leisure time has become an important consideration in the use of an individual's time. The traditional student of the community college is becoming more difficult to define. The average age of the student today is reaching the upper 20s which indicates a need on the part of the institution to design more non-traditional delivery systems for the vocational-technical programs, general education courses and the adult and continuing education, or leisure-time courses.

Keeping a finger on the pulse of the marketplace is important and a necessary task of the community college if it is to remain a vital solution to the needs of the community it serves. The structure of the institution must be designed to be flexible and efficient, while at the same time cost-effective for the student. Steps should be taken to reach out into the community and make more effective use of the linkages between business and industry and the community colleges. Resources exist both on campus as well as off campus for the institution that is willing to make the investment of time to seek them out.

The step into the unknown of the future can be a more certain one if the faculty and staff of the organization can better understand where they fit into the mission of the institution and are prepared to take the necessary steps to affect changes. The future of the community college remains in its ability to design effective structural changes to better enable it to meet its changing mission.

ABOUT THE AUTHOR

ELEANOR OTT is President of Eastfield
College, Dallas County Community College
District. Formerly she has served in the
capacities of Vice President of Student
Services and Vice President of Instruction
as well as Dean of Student Services, counselor, and instructor at other colleges. A
member of the board of a hospital, chamber
of commerce, Goodwill Industries and a
bank, Ott is also a national panelist for the
National Endowment for the Humanities
and the American Council on Education.
She is also the author of several journal
articles.

10
Student Services Programs: A Second Look

Eleanor Ott

Student services departments and activities have been and still are key elements in community colleges. These units have designed their activities and programs in response to student needs, attempting to alter and modify them as expressed needs have changed. The swings and sways within the effort have been reflective of many elements: current student achievement levels, the women's movement, the aging of American society, returning veterans, heightened awareness of special interest groups, predominate values, changing roles within the family unit, redefinition of the family itself, and on and on.

At best, while it has not been easy, it has not been impossible to design programs responding to needs, chiefly because they have been identifiable and have appeared at a reasonable pace. Yet in 1965 the American Association of Community and Junior Colleges/Carnegie report described student services functions as being "woefully inadequate." This same report noted that the traditional functions of admissions, orientation, and counseling were neither uniformly integrated nor were they adequately supported. The addition of other kinds of services undertaken by this group of professionals could not have improved this evaluation. A compounding problem is the identity crisis which the evolution of these supplemental functions has produced for the student personnel movement. Elsner and Ames relate a descriptive story which highlights the problem.

> At a faculty meeting, one of the faculty members said that it was disconcerting for him to see so many specialists with names and job descriptions which, on the face of their job description, it was impossible to tell what they did. He said, "I am a teacher of English. People know what I do and where I do it and, generally, how I do it."[1]

Nor does the era itself offer assistance. The bestselling author and forecaster, John Naisbitt, outlines a confounding factor, when he says that, "We are living in a time of the parenthesis, the time between eras," and describes the situation in this manner:

> It is as though we have bracketed off the past and the future, for we are neither here or there. We have not quite left behind the either/or America of the past—but we have not embraced the future either. We have done the human thing; we are clinging to the known past in fear of the unknown future. Those who are willing to handle the ambiguity of this in-between period and to anticipate the new era will be a quantum leap ahead of those who hold on to the past. The time of the parenthesis is a time of change and questioning.[2]

In this time of change and questioning, surely no group faces more difficult inquiries about their work and even their value than the student service worker. Is it because their efforts are no longer as important to the educational experience as it once was? Is it a matter of tight money establishing the college's priorities? Or is it that the professional abilities exhibited by student personnel workers are no longer important?

Paul Elsner and W. Clark Ames recently suggested that the principal reason for the current precarious position of student services programs is because of the inability of these workers to document the impact of their services upon students. These authors suggest that student services personnel have been unable to identify the "coin of their realm" or successfully determine whether they are supplemental to the instructional program or full partners with it.

Information presently available about the numbers of student services programs eliminated because of budget restrictions indicates that for the most part student services departments are seen as peripheral to the instructional efforts. However, at the same time, when future trends are examined, a set of definable student needs emerges which are of the type only student personnel staff can address adequately.

Elsner and Ames cluster responses to these needs into several distinct categories:

1. Institutionally based services.

2. Situationally based services.

3. Special interest and/or developmental services.

These authors define institutionally based services as those which provide basic processing and record-keeping services and situationally based services as including those such as health services, student activities, housing, etc. The difficult member of this group to define is the special interest and/or development services. These services are tied to both special interests and developmental needs of students and include programs for the underprepared minorities, programs for re-entry women, and other programs for specific groups like the handicapped and senior adults.

In light of current thinking, it is this group of special interests and/or developmental services which provides the greatest options for the future. For example, John Naisbitt describes a set of needs which are direct responses to the contemporary technological invasion we are experiencing. He suggests that there has been an evolution of a highly personal value system as compensation for the impersonal nature of technology. Naisbitt believes technology and the personal growth movement are interlocked. His phrase "high tech/high touch" describes this relationship. Naisbitt states that, "Now at the dawn of the twenty-first century, high tech/high touch truly has come of age. Technology and our human potential are the two great challenges and adventures facing humankind today. The great lesson we must learn from the principle of high tech/high touch is a modern version of the ancient Greek ideal of balance."

Colleges across the country are scrambling to offer students as much high tech training as they can manage. Sophisticated equipment is being purchased and liaisons with industry are being forged in order to realize this goal. Yet, as schedules are being expanded to accommodate the students clammering for high tech training, it is difficult to discover comparable increases in human development or human potential courses. Nor is it possible to detect an interest on the part of those teaching technical courses to incorporate human development learning objectives into their offerings. On the contrary, pressure is coming from faculty and community advisors to clean up the curriculum and clear out the "frills." At the same time, while indicators point to a need for generalists who can adapt, we see more specialized education being requested and offered.

These changing times seem to be producing both the best and the worst for student services professionals. Future-oriented people identify student needs which these groups are trained to fulfill. Yet, it is difficult to discover a community college which has dedicated the budget necessary to implement the programs to meet these needs.

When student services staffs reconceptualize their missions, when they become clear about services they can deliver, and when they can clearly state how their human potential expertise supports technology, they will have taken a major step forward.

A different type of opportunity for student personnel workers is reported by Elsner and Ames in their description of a project between the Rio Salado Community College and the Motorola Corporation. This project has successfully reduced a full two-year program into a one-year, intensive course of instruction accompanied by a variety of student service support functions. The program was designed to take Motorola workers, many of whom were women and minorities, off the assembly line and prepare them for more advanced positions in the semi-conductor processing and electronics divisions of the company.

Elsner and Ames report that the first attempts to put this program in place were nearly disastrous. The developers of the program are quick to state that it is easy to put together a 52-week program and to conceptualize it and modularize it on paper, but difficult to implement it successfully.

When the program was initiated, a great deal of stress was experienced by the students in the program. The students indicated that courses such as English 101, Chemistry, Introduction to Algebra, and other demanding academic subjects were not being taught by qualified instructors. The instructors, they said, should be removed and replaced by others. Soon after the first few weeks, the students indicated that they felt this was some kind of trick or scheme on the part of management to push them into a program that led more to their failure and agony than to any chance for success at the end of the program.

During the fifth and sixth weeks, the students began to turn on each other. Leaders and instructors noticed a high degree of irritability, much peer pressure, squabbling, quarreling, etc. In a very short period of time, not too long into the semester, the program almost disintegrated. A gifted counselor and advisor, who had worked with the program from the beginning, conducted emergency and crisis sessions. The counselor managed to calm the students, as well as the training director and the college staff, so that the program would move forward.

As a solution, courses in reducing math anxiety, increasing self-awareness, developing coping strategies, and building teams were taught during the first two weeks, but the students' frustrations still developed. The frustrations were first directed at teachers, next to the employer, and families, and then to each other. The role of the counselor, serving as a human development specialist, a teacher, a buffer, a translator and a release valve, has begun to be realized. Initial surveys have been implemented to assess the personal growth of each individual, specialized tutoring has been provided; but, so much more needs to be explored. We have learned, according to the project director, that the "flow chart is not the person; it is the person in the program who must succeed if the model is to work."

In the redesign of the program, the developers quickly admitted that their original design simply did not include enough support services for industry-selected participants moved into a college class setting. In the words of one of the program directors, "The complex marginalized lives of the assembly line worker, now turned full-time student, has tremendous impact for support services."

There is little doubt that a large part of the future of the community college as a whole is going to be tied to how effectively that institution works with industry. The success of efforts such as those described between Rio Salado and Motorola point out the need for college support systems to be fully integrated with student progress. The integration of human development elements into the mainstream of the instructional process is an absolute necessity if we hope to preserve what has been described as our greatest natural resource, human productivity.

Within a community college, only student personnel workers can deliver the programs necessary to reach the goal of assisting students with preparation for an uncertain future. The rational response to inquiries about whether or not student services professionals are needed for the future is a resounding, "more than ever." In answering that call, two requirements become clear. Student services professionals must reconceptualize their roles in such a way that, 1) their contributions become not only integral elements in the instructional process but also, 2) are recognized as being instruction in and of itself.

How can SPOD professionals assist in this process? The challenge begs an action response.

REFERENCES

[1] Elsner, P. A., Ames, W. C. 1983 Draft of a chapter submitted for publication in a forthcoming book by George B. Vaughn entitled, *The Community College: Alternative Perspectives.*

[2] Naisbitt, J. 1982 *Megatrends: Ten New Directions Transforming Our Lives*. Warner Books, New York.

ABOUT THE AUTHORS

JOYCE S. TSUNODA is Chancellor for Community Colleges, University of Hawaii and holds a Ph.D. degree in Bio-chemistry. Former positions held include Acting Assistant Vice-President for Academic Affairs, University of Hawaii System and Provost, Kapiolani Community College. Tsunoda is a Board member of the National Center for Higher Education Management Systems and the American Council on Education. She is a member of the Western Association of Schools and Colleges Appeals Hearing Board Panel and Secretary/Treasurer of the Private Industry Council of the City and County of Honolulu. A former Board member of AACJC, she was also a member of the Advisory Council on Developing Instututions, Office of Education, Department of Health, Education and Welfare.

MARVIN VEREGGE (photo unavailable), is Coordinator of the state staff development program for community colleges and formerly was a counselor at colleges in Hawaii and California.

11
Hawaii's Community College's Hui Kūkākūkā

Joyce Tsunoda and Marvin Veregge

"Hui kūkākūkā" is a Hawaiian phrase meaning gathering together, gathering together for the purpose of discussing and solving problems. "Gathering Together" represents the theme of one of Hawaii's Community Colleges' major thrusts in staff development, a colloquium series; and, it describes the approach used by administration, faculty and staff to solve some of Hawaii's unique problems in this area, as well.

The rapid growth and management of staff development in Hawaii has not been so much the result of a rational quantitative approach to problem solving, but rather, as Peters and Waterman suggest in their book *In Search of Excellence*, "a commitment too difficult to measure things like people and quality." The program shares many of the attributes of excellence Peters and Waterman describe: "a bias for action; closeness to the customer (i.e. the administrators, faculty or staff members for whom the activities are designed); belief in productivity through people; a hands-on value driven operation; autonomy at the lowest levels; a tendency to stick to the knitting; and a simple form and lean staff." In retrospect, Hawaii has used a dash of "quality circles," a pinch of "Theory Z," and large amounts of "grass-roots determination" all mixed with generous heapings of "aloha" to create a staff development model for the future.

HAWAII'S COMMUNITY COLLEGES – 19 YEARS YOUNG

Hawaii's Community Colleges are young by mainland standards. When the 1964 State Legislature enacted legislation establishing community colleges, it mandated a system of community colleges under the authority of the Board of Regents of the University of Hawaii. The University of Hawaii Community College System includes seven colleges. Four colleges (Honolulu, Kapiolani, Leeward and Windward) are located on the island of Oahu while the other three are located on the islands from which they take their name (Maui, Kauai, and Hawaii). Maui Community College also services the islands of Lanai and Molokai.

The community college system, headed by a chancellor for community colleges, constitutes a system within the university system. Each community college is headed by a provost who reports to the chancellor for community colleges, who in turn serves under the president of the University of Hawaii. The exception to this is the provost of Hawaii Community College who reports to the chancellor of the University of Hawaii at Hilo. Operating and capital improvement funds for the entire University of Hawaii System are derived through appropriation by the state legislature. University revenues, such as tuition, are returned to the state general fund.

STAFF DEVELOPMENT ROOTS

Hawaii's community colleges share with their mainland counterparts a history of rapid, well-financed growth in the sixties and seventies followed by slower growth and the budget "crunch" of the eighties. Although a comparatively new system, by the beginning of the seventies concern arose over how to assist the rising percentage of tenured faculty in meeting the ever changing, post-secondary educational needs of the state's population and economy. Each college was requested by the board of regents to prepare a comprehensive Faculty/Staff Renewal and Vitality Plan. Since little activity occurred as a result of their request, in the summer of 1980 the board of regents developed and approved a comprehensive Faculty/Staff Renewal and Vitality Policy. Unfortunately, at the same time the board also announced it was considering adopting a policy requiring periodic review of all board of regents appointees. This review policy was viewed by many faculty as a threat to tenure. Suspicion arose that staff development plans might become tied to faculty evaluation. It was during this era of distrust and some hostility that the "Gathering Together" approach to staff development came into being.

In August of 1980, Dewey Kim, then chancellor for the community colleges, organized a special task force, composed of representatives from each campus, to develop a system-wide policy, activities plan, coordination and organizational framework, and budgeting process for staff development which would include campus-based and system-wide activities. Upon completion of its draft, the task force organized an all-day conference for 130 community college administrators, faculty and staff to discuss the document and implementation of a system-wide staff development plan. As a result to this conference, it was agreed that in order to have a viable staff development program, evaluation of faculty and staff would have to be handled separately. The final draft underwent extensive review by each campus.

By July 1981 a comprehensive, staff development plan for the community colleges had been set in place. The chancellor's approach of involving all levels of staff in the initial planning and organization began to dispel some of the "fears" of a board-mandated policy on staff development; and, each college set about with renewed enthusiasm to develop its own campus Faculty/Staff Renewal and Vitality Plan geared to the needs and unique features of the individual college.

Organization and leadership for staff development has grown from the grass-roots campus level upward. Some colleges have formed college-wide staff development committees while others have appointed coordinators for each group to be served (i.e. administration, faculty, clerical, operations and maintenance, etc.). Almost all colleges have selected a person, usually a full-time faculty member with released time, to serve as a college's coordinator of staff development. System-wide coordination is provided by a full-time coordinator of staff development in the chancellor for community colleges' office. To date, this position has been filled by rotating faculty members from the various colleges into the position every one or two years. The advantages of this co-ordinating approach at the system's level is that it provides "internship" experience in the chancellor's office and a system-wide perspective for those who participate. Salary costs for the system coordinator are shared between the campus providing the faculty member and the chancellor's office.

Each college determines, executes, and funds those staff development activities which it feels are most appropriate to its needs. Campus coordinators meet monthly with the system coordinator to share activities and ideas as well as plan system-wide staff development efforts.

STAFF DEVELOPMENT IN AN ISLAND STATE

Although Hawaii faces almost all of the universal problems of staff development, its geographical location and island character have added some problems which are unique. Not only is Hawaii isolated from the mainland, but the four major islands are isolated from one another as well. Where a distance of 50 to 100 miles may be easily traversed on the mainland, movement of staff members from one island to another for workshops or in-service training involves considerable planning and expense in Hawaii. Perhaps even more important, living on an island creates a "psychological set" of being isolated, one from the other. In addition, or perhaps as an outgrowth of its isolation, Hawaii has traditionally sought to hire and promote from within as a means of minimizing the out-migration of its population. Although Hawaii's community colleges' staff are well prepared, there is not the constant infusion of new ideas and approaches often gained from "new outside or mainland hires." The prohibitive costs of sending large numbers of staff to mainland conferences or constantly bringing in "consultants" has forced the community colleges to seek alternative solutions to the problems of feelings of isolation and the need to constantly update and upgrade staff expertise.

NEEDS ASSESSMENT

As part of its fact finding activities, the chancellor's task force had conducted a system-wide needs assessment. Every community college staff member from custodian to provost was polled to determine his or her views on staff development needs. The response was overwhelming: "We want to get together to discuss what we are doing and how to solve our common problems." Although vocational educators from all islands had traditionally met for in-service training over the years, little had been done to facilitate communications and joint problem solving among liberal arts faculty and no effort had been made to bring clerical, business office or maintenance staffs together. Here was a thrust for staff development which promised to tap the existing expertise within the community college system, maximize knowledge gained by the few from mainland conferences, provide for meaningful dialog and joint problem solving at the level of problem involvement and reduce feelings of isolation as well. Perhaps most important, it was an approach that grew out of the real needs and desires of those for whom staff development activities were intended. From this simple suggestion has grown the Chancellor's Colloquim Series, "Gathering Together."

THE COLLOQUIUM SERIES

The primary assumption of the colloquium series was the recognition that significant improvement in instruction and in the learning environment for students can be assured only by an informed and vital teaching faculty. Since faculty are primarily responsible for the development of curriculum on campus, peer interaction and the fostering of a system-wide focus can encourage creativity and flexibility in instruction that will improve the learning environment for students.

The primary goals were: (1) to provide teaching faculty with the opportunity to gain information on the significant projects in curriculum development and evaluation completed and in progress in the Hawaii Community College System; (2) to identify common existing shifting student populations, and focus on students with special needs (handicapped, displaced homemakers, developmentally disabled, etc); (3) to begin the development of an active system-wide faculty network to facilitate intra-campus dialogue, and to recommend a mechanism for systematizing inter-campus sharing of resources, faculty exchanges, and professional activities; (4) to provide special opportunity for neighbor island faculty to improve peer interaction often denied them because of geographical isolation; and, (5) to make recommendations on current projects and future plans.

Each academic year, faculty representing all major disciplines in the community college system have the opportunity to meet for a one- or two-day session with their peers to discuss and make recommendations on some significant aspects of curriculum development and/or evaluation that affect the system as a whole. Some groups were asked, for part of their sessions, to take up issues already identified in the chancellor's objectives for 1980-81 and the system's long-range planning document, *Direction for the 80s.* Each group had the opportunity to create an agenda to identify and discuss their own topics. Each session had a host campus and a colloquium coordinator to work with faculty in the planning of an agenda and format. In large-discipline or multi-discipline areas, groups met together or separately.

As no funds had been budgeted for the activity, the chancellor submitted the colloquim series proposal to the U. H. president's Educational Improvement Fund Committee. An award of $3,000 was provided to conduct the program for the balance of the academic year. Fourteen colloquia in general education and six in vocational education were held between March 23 and May 19, 1981. Over 455 faculty and staff participated. Every campus hosted at least one colloquium and 124 neighbor island faculty joined their peers on Oahu.

Each colloquium had been the outgrowth of a request by a given discipline or faculty group. Faculty volunteered to serve as conveners and resource persons. All planning, setting of agendas, chairing colloquium sessions and reporting of results and recommendations was done by the participants. The chancellor's office coordinated details, provided travel funds and assembled the final year-end report. In addition to the enthusiastic response and well-thought-out recommendations in curriculum improvement and articulation one thing was clear, the series needed to be continued and expanded.

As a result of the enthusiasm generated by the initial series, the colleges allocated additional funds for staff development. Travel expenses were jointly shared by the colleges, the chancellor's office and, in many instances, by the participants, themselves. In 1982, 720 faculty and staff "gathered together" in 16 different colloquia. For the first time, at their request, meetings for clerical and support staff were included.

The series was threatened in 1983 when the governor "froze" all travel funds mid-year in response to impending state deficits. This time the chancellor appealed to the University of Hawaii Foundation for funds and another $3,000 was awarded to continue the program. Nineteen colloquia were held involving 584 participants.

"Gathering Together" is no longer strictly a faculty, staff development activity. What was once a set colloquium series has expanded to include a wide variety of workshops and meetings, such as the workshop for business office personnel to discuss and problem-solve new university requirements in purchase order procedures, a two-day seminar for clerical staff on "Renewing Ourselves and Our Institutions," and meetings of operations personnel on how to improve energy conservation methods.

CREATIVE FINANCING

To suggest Hawaii's problems are well on their way to solution would be absurd. Budgets keep getting tighter and staff development, particularly travel, funds are prime candidates for "trimming." Again this year the chancellor must seek extramural funding for the colloquium series through the University of Hawaii Foundation. However, true to the spirit of "hui kūkākūkā," administrators, faculty and staff in every college have gathered together to find alternative methods of supplementing lean staff development budgets. Three colleges (Kauai, Maui and Leeward) have set up college advancement funds through the University of Hawaii Foundation. The colleges solicit funds from business, community organizations and individuals within the general and college community. Employees of the colleges are encouraged to participate in a payroll deduction plan to add to the advancement fund. Last year one college even sponsored a "huli huli" (local method of barbeque) chicken sale to provide funds for staff development through its college advancement fund. In each case, the funds are monitored and administered by college-wide committees to insure the most worthy staff development activities are funded. A yearly John Fry [1] Memorial Seminar in staff development has been funded by individual contributions from the various colleges' staff to honor the memory of one of Hawaii's pioneers in this field. Other approaches to funding have been the use of AIDP, Title III, and Vocational Education funds and NSF projects.

EXPLORING THE FUTURE

A host of individual and campus activities, system-wide workshops and the colloquium series are marks of the present. Each time staff members gather together they are already planning the future. One area being explored is how to tie staff development into long-range planning. The community college system has a long-range planning document, *Direction for the 80s*. Each college has an educational development plan and a faculty/staff renewal and vitality plan as well as its biennium budget. Now the task is to merge these planning documents to insure a well planned staff development program and yet keep the spontaneity and grass roots approach. Further, staff members from all islands are exploring the feasibility of telecommunication conferences with each other, the mainland and our sister islands of the South Pacific. The momentum engendered by "Gathering Together" appears

---

[1] John Fry started at Leeward Community College as an instructor in history and became the first coordinator of a staff development program in a Hawaii community college. His last position, before his untimely death due to cancer, was as Director of Community Services, Kapiolani Community College. John was an active member of NCSPOD and was the one individual who introduced NCSPOD to Hawaii. He organized Hawaii's chapter (HASPOD), and served as a vital link between Hawaii and the mainland on staff development. His legacy still lives on in Hawaii.

to be spreading throughout the community college system. For example, the community college historians are raising funds to support bringing in visiting historians while philosophers are establishing a formal organization to increase communications within their group. Everywhere, one senses an eagerness to grow and move forward by creative problem solving.

Although our tradition looks down on "bragging," Hawaii's community colleges are justly proud of their accomplishments to date. What has evolved was not rationally planned in an administrator's office but something that grew out of the determination of the staff at all levels to improve the quality of their own performance. Indeed, it has been action oriented, simple in form and lean on staff. But, throughout there has been the belief in the people who work so hard to serve the educational needs of our community. Perhaps, Hawaii's experience can serve as a model for some of our sister institutions. We offer it in the spirit of aloha and "hui kūkākūkā."

ABOUT THE AUTHOR

BILL F. STEWART holds a Doctor of Education degree and is President of Kirkwood Community College, Cedar Rapids, Iowa. He has worked in community college administration in two other states as well. He served as President of Anchorage Community College in Alaska as well as Associate Dean of Student Services and Student Activities, Dean of Community Education, and Vice President of the District Centers Program at Mt. Hood Community College in Oregon. He is a member of the Board of the American Council on Education, AACJC, the League for Innovation in the Community College, Cooperative for the Advancement of Community-Based Post-Secondary Education and Community Colleges for International Development.

12
The Impact of Educational Technology on Staff Development Programs

Bill F. Stewart

Educators cannot rely on crystal ball gazing nor on intuitive speculation about the future and the role that the new technology will play in our professional lives. The rapid changes taking place in science and society are directly reflected in our own programs and institutional organizations. As the insightful poet Alfred Lord Tennyson stated in his historical work *The Passing of Arthur*, "The old order changeth, yielding place to new." We are experiencing a cycle of change in our lives so rapid that it would amaze that nineteenth century sage, yet we must meet this challenge with confidence and creativity.

We ask ourselves what impact this change is having on education in general, and specifically the community college system in America. What "new order" is now evident and how do we keep pace with the technological advances that explode around us?

During the past decade, community colleges have emerged as a powerful arm of higher education. The 1,200 community, technical and junior colleges located throughout this country now serve over ten million students. They continue to do so in a cost-effective, qualitative manner while recognizing and allowing for fluctuating job market trends and the changing needs of the people served.

At the core of dramatic changes in technology, economy, and our culture are people—a fact that should never be forgotten or dismissed. Within our own organizations we must remain accountable to our students, with their diverse competencies and aspirations; our faculty, who maintain the highest quality of instruction; and our staff and managers, all striving to provide the necessary support services while managing increasingly limited resources.

Amidst the dynamism of change should come the reaffirmation of the human element. As we learn to adapt to and embrace the changing technology, we must also provide for the comparable changes in people. As Alvin Toffler noted in the *Third Wave:*

> As Third Wave civilization matures, we shall create not a utopian man or woman who towers over the people of the past, not a superhuman race . . . but merely, and proudly one hopes, a race—and a civilization—that deserves to be called human.

And, concludes Toffler,

> Above all, they (the individuals of the future) seem likely to crave balance in their lives—balance between work and play, between headwork and handwork, between the abstract and the concrete, between objectivity and subjectivity.

Toffler's emphasis, of course, is on the development of the whole person, and it is the development of the whole person that is the priority of a sound educational staff development program. Community colleges are in an enviable position to not only keep pace with, but to lead in the training and development of our staff members, as well as those employees of neighboring businesses and industrial firms.

Kirkwood Community College has developed and implemented several unique programs which serve our faculty and staff as well as providing training to members of the general educational and business community. Under our Community Education Division, our goal is to provide a seminar per day, and that goal has long since been reached as we now average

an offering of one hundred seminars per month. The populari-
ty of our programs reflects the hunger for knowledge and
training in advanced fields of technology. From the use of
microcomputers to assertiveness training, the programs are
continually drawing record numbers of registrations.

Kirkwood employees are encouraged to participate in
classes, workshops, and seminars as a basic component of our
staff development program. By allowing for no-fee or low-fee
attendance, this is a cost effective method of bringing a major
training resource to our own back door.

The highest priority identified by staff members in determining the direction of our development program was that of
computer literacy. Employees may enroll in formal data processing courses where reserved spaces are available for staff.
They may enroll in non-credit community education courses
in the computer area, or they may choose to learn indepen-
dently by using training modules developed for use in our
computer literacy laboratory. Knowledge of computer capability is an all-encompassing college goal, and the entire staff
will have the opportunity to become comfortable, if not
highly competent, in this area during the current academic
year if they so desire.

Being a pioneer in interactive microwave telecommunications as an educational delivery system has brought more
than notoriety to the Kirkwood campus. Along with the
highly technical equipment component of the program came
the "human" side of the system. This included adaptation
and revision of curriculum and instructional methodologies
and the development of compatible programs. It also became
imperative to train our faculty and technicians to use the system effectively. The following is a brief overview of the
major aspects of the Kirkwood Telecommunications Systems.

The Kirkwood Telecommunications System provides a
variety of interactive telecommunications services. The external delivery portion of the system includes interactive microwave (telelinks) interconnecting eight locations, Instructional Television Fixed Service (ITFS) which includes four
main channels of operation at the Kirkwood campus site and
six additional channels at various transmitter sites throughout
Kirkwood's seven-county service area, two channels of educational access cable, origination classrooms, a telecommunica-

tions control center, and a 10,000 watt public radio station.

The term "Telelink" is used to identify each of the seven point-to-point microwave links connecting Kirkwood classrooms in outlying communities with the main campus. In day-to-day operation, this allows students to enroll in classes right in their home communities, saving time and travel expenses, while still being able to participate in face-to-face discussions with their instructors and with other students. In operation, some of Kirkwood's Telelinks are carrying a portion of the college's voice communications, and they soon will give students at outlying sites access via terminals to the library card catalog, computer-assisted instruction lessons, and a variety of other data support services.

ITFS, or Instructional Television Fixed Service, is a form of broadcast television which can be picked up by special dish antennas and receivers from any line-of-site point within a twenty-mile radius of the transmitting tower. ITFS provides both audio and video outgoing transmission, as well as an audio return response from any receiver site. Four ITFS channels are broadcast from the Kirkwood main campus. Programming being developed for the ITFS service in Kirkwood's district includes the following:

- Live and recorded courses for credit, continuing education and community education for civic groups, local agencies, professional organizations, and citizens of the outlying communities.

- A secondary school service channel delivering live instruction or special presentations, and feeding films, tapes, and other recorded support materials directly to area schools for immediate use or later playback.

- A business and industrial service channel presenting live and recorded educational programming designed especially for employees in large and small factories and businesses in the area, programming which can be received directly in the plant or place of business.

Kirkwood operates a full service educational channel on the community cable system. Among the programs on Channel 13 are these:

- Live interactive credit courses originating on campus.

(Students at home can dial a local telephone number to talk directly to the instructor or class.)

- Recorded telecourses offered for those watching at home.

- Live and recorded special programs and events.

- Film and videotape general educational and cultural programs from local and national sources.

- Information about Kirkwood.

The TV Distribution System is a 36-channel on-campus cable TV network connecting individual classrooms, shops, and labs in all permanent classroom buildings with a single feedpoint known as the TV Distribution Center. Permanently stored in the center are about 4,000 instructional programs on videotape, along with all equipment to feed these programs to all areas of the campus by cable, and intercom telephone system, and a staff of system operators whose job it is to lead and play the programs requested by students and staff. The TV Distribution System operates totally on a demand-access basis with no scheduling, no reserved tapes, and no censorship. A person typically can begin viewing a program within 30 seconds of having picked up the phone to request it. Access is free and totally anonymous. The system operates fourteen hours per day.

A three-member team was established to address the technical aspect of electronic learning, as well as the staff and program development concerns, and the marketing and implementation in the off-campus sites throughout our seven-county service area. These three administrators work closely together to insure a comprehensive plan that maintains the necessary balance between "people" and "machines."

Training faculty to use the new interactive telecommunications system was not left to chance. A formal in-service program was developed to acquaint faculty members with the simplicity of the system as well as the more complex and technical aspects. Every attempt was made to make the process non-threatening and to build faculty confidence as they approached a new instructional setting. In-service sessions addressed how to plan and prepare for classes, classroom management techniques, use of media and equipment and how

to enjoy the unique experience of teaching to "distant learners." We began to realize how seriously the faculty members
viewed the success of this venture when their grooming and
attire improved along with their planning and instructional
skills. This well-developed program included follow-up,
periodic review, and continual monitoring so that only the
highest quality of instruction is delivered over the system.

The telecommunications system has also allowed Kirkwood to become a provider of staff development for local
businesses and K-12 school districts. Coursework can be
provided in a local community school facility via the Instructional Television Fixed Service (ITFS) arrangement. Training
in local business and industrial sites can also be made possible
over the ITFS linkages. Of special note is the possibility of
training engineers and hospital personnel in their own work-
sites with the instruction originating from the University of
Iowa in nearby Iowa City. The training implications for highly
technical industries using such a high-tech delivery system is
staggering. The extent of its use depends upon human need,
ingenuity in programming, and acceptance by training professionals and their staffs. As Russell Edgerton, president of
the American Association for Higher Education, noted in
Meeting Learners' Needs Through Telecommunications:

> During the 50s, 60s, and 70s, we learned to wince at the
> periodic—and false—proclamations that technology was about
> to revolutionize higher education. But now, the 80s have ar-
> rived, and we are waking up to the fact that it's really happen-
> ing; this decade *is* going to be different.

Certainly that difference has been evident in the expanded
program opportunities and accompanying support services
which have been brought to learners through use of interactive
microwave, cable television, radio and the telephone. Clearly
in sight, but still on the horizon, is the use of technology to
serve a wide variety of constituencies simultaneously; that
is, for staff development purposes through a coordinated
system of activities and resources that would provide for local
in-service as well as to reach nationwide. Staff development
could easily be provided via a system of six to eight national
dissemination centers which could be the agencies for a

variety of telecommunications activities and events. There is every reason to believe that components of a sophisticated, comprehensive staff development program could be made accessible to any, or all, of the community colleges in the country through cooperation and technical linkages.

Of course, there are complexities involved in mounting such an extensive network. But, as Louis Robinson, director of the Scientific Computing Division of IBM, states, "The challenge really lies in applying the technology to the human welfare, to our institutions, even our businesses, so that we may somehow, directly or indirectly, affect and improve the human condition."

The future of staff development partially lies in the willingness of administrators to capitalize on the new technologies, for faculty and staff to become directly involved in the efforts, and for the public to perceive and support the need for systematic, on-going professional and personal development programs. Above all, the future rests with employers who are concerned with the overall welfare of their employees and who recognize that a comprehensive staff development program is not only humanistic, but a wise investment in human resources.

Peters and Waterman remind us in their book, *In Search of Excellence*, that characteristics of successful businesses include: 1) respecting individuals, for they are the root source of productivity and quality; 2) fostering leadership and innovation; and 3) offering opportunities to celebrate together. Well-designed, quality staff development programs that merge the human element with modern technological delivery systems can be a way for professionals to "grow" and to "celebrate" together.

SECTION TWO
Advocacy, Predictions, and Aspirations: Future Trends Commission Foci

ABOUT THE AUTHOR

PATRICIA C. BRAMS holds a doctors degree in education and is presently Staff and Instructional Specialist for the 2,000 employees of the Houston Community College System. She has served as Visiting Assistant Professor at Rice University and as Lecturer for three years at Njala University College, Sierra Leone, West Africa. She has published numerous articles and consulted here and abroad in the areas of modernity, international development and education, social change and American education, instructional design, educational planning, advocacy and staff development. Brams is a member of the American Society for Training and Development and the Texas Council for Staff, Professional, and Organizational Development.

13
Shaping the Future:
Educators As Futurists
and Advocates

Patricia Brams

Traditionally, education is defined as the process through which children are socialized to identify with their historical roots and are prepared to function productively in contemporary society. The context of education is the past and present, transmitting what is already known with the goal of fitting students into the established social pattern. Adult education is hardly different. Community colleges, for example, offer occupational training for immediate placement in the workplace and lifelong learning geared to the immediate needs and interests of their clientele. Learning, likewise, is defined narrowly in terms of past and present, most often as measurable "pretest-posttest" changes in behavior acquired in the short run rather than as a fundamental broadening of perspective with insights into the élan of past to present social transformation as a precursor of the future. Ironic indeed that educators whose profession targets those members of society who will be closest to the cutting edge of tomorrow should be solidly centered on yesterday and today; not surprising that those they teach are also oriented mainly to the quotidian.

Fortunately, the situation is not hopeless. We live in a

capacious, rapidly changing era--an era of uncertainty and challenge. We are experiencing a "paradigm shift," a time of global transition and pervasive, formidable change in our values, technology, insitutions and lifestyles. Problems are proliferating, critical and unique. Creativity, analysis, experience, judgment and advocacy are required to meet the swell of the "third wave."[1] For educators, this constitutes an unusual opportunity. Not only does a transition tend to marshal talent from new quarters to garner solutions to urgent problems, but there is now a groundswell of particular interest in the future of education and a renewed public awareness of the connection between education and economic productivity, political efficacy and quality of future lifestyles.

If ever there were an ideal time for educators to assume leadership in forging the future, it is now. No longer is education relegated to perpetuate the past and provide for the present. A part of the future is being set aside as the domain of educators; they have finally been included in a territory formerly reserved for politicians, economists, and technologists. Can we meet the challenge of this new role which demands vision, proaction, and the highest order of intellectual and communication skills to guide the course of our national and global destinies?

The purposes of this paper are: 1) to present a brief overview of the concerns and techniques of the futures field to provide educators a sense of the mindset and skills required to address the future; 2) to offer a model of communication plan to enable educators to impact the future as public informers, change agents and advocates; and, 3) to outline specific means by which SPOD practitioners, administrators, and state and national organizations can become proactive in shaping the future.

THE FUTURES FIELD: EDUCATORS AS FUTURISTS

The futures field is an emerging discipline concerned with the study of what is possible, probable and preferable in the future. Futurists attempt to describe alternate paths for global development (the possible), to determine which is likely (the probable) and to consider which paths are desirable (the preferable), working to implement them.[2]

Futurists concerned with the possible are intuitive and visionary, often geniuses and writers with fresh and compelling imagination. They brainstorm uncharted paths into the future. Those concerned with the probable future, on the other hand, are analytical. They observe trends and extrapolate the qualitative and quantitative consequences of the extension of one or several integrated trends over time. Futurists concerned with the preferable deal with "educating people to help them discover and choose intelligently, involving those who will be affected by likely developments and choices in the decision-making process, winning support for perferred alternatives and choices, and helping to bring about change."[3]

The role of the educator as futurist is to deal with the preferable, to utilize futures field projections of what is possible and probable and to educate, persuade and stimulate public dialogue, promoting consensus and action to implement choices. Educators need not become futurists using systems analysis, operations research, Delphi, path analysis, gaming and conflict resolution in the manner of futurists, but should become accustomed to approach problems with a sense of the interrelatedness of education to other aspects of societal flux and to project and assess the future impact of current decisions. Succinctly, the educator, using the futures field as a resource, can "image, analyze and participate" in creating the future, using educational issues and problems as initial foci.[4]

From the futures field, educators can adopt: 1) an attitude of openness and imaginative freedom; 2) a conceptual, if not operative, understanding of futurists' analytical techniques; 3) the use of systems theory and induction and deduction to project present circumstance to future outcomes and to work backwards from an ideal future to determine required present action; and, 4) modes to evaluate choices and to advocate acceptance.

COMMUNICATION: EDUCATORS AS ADVOCATES

The futures field suggests new approaches to address educational issues in the context of social planning. Communication theory provides a model to enable educators to communicate with other educators, lay public and government to provide information, clarify issues, and advocate choices which will have favorable outcomes in the future. Education is essentially a process of communication so it is certainly appropriate for educators to support futurists by communicating their concerns and activating the public to become better informed, more proactive and prospective in decision-making.

To be effective advocates, educators must enlarge their view of themselves as informers, advocates and change agents. To be effective, they should design plans to communicate information based on a model which includes four basic components: audience, medium, message, and strategy. Specific options for each component should be selected so that medium, message, and strategy are appropriate for a particular audience. The goal of communication is to inform the audience of the issue and to stimulate interest and discussion. This will hopefully lead to enlightened public policy. Dialogue affords an opportunity to clarify and examine ideas to resolve differences of opinion. Acceptance of ideas is facilitated through personal interactions.[5]

The outcome of public dialogue will not necessarily result in consensus, but well-planned communication that emphasizes the relationship of the issue to personal well-being and survival may indeed compel the majority to act in favor of decisions which will ensure favorable future outcomes.

Audience

The first consideration in developing a communication plan is the selection of an audience. Educators have access to diverse audiences, some of which include students, colleagues, professional organizations, leaders in government, international organizations, and community groups. Educators may communicate to individuals or groups with whom they are already established, or they may become active on committees and task forces in professional and civic groups to extend the scope of their influence. Collaboration with social scientists in other disciplines allows contact with a broad interdisciplinary audience.

In some instances, they may not need to seek an audience

but will be sought by the media or as consultants. At other times, they may volunteer to speak on educational issues in their institutions and communities. They may inform their students or even run for public office to gain a position of leadership to promote judicious educational planning.

This array of possibilities enables educators to plan for broad and far-reaching impact. More important than the size of the audiences is that educators feel comfortable with the audience and are credible advocates for that particular audience. Furthermore, they must be able to adapt their communication techniques to the age, culture, sex, attitudes, beliefs, values, and interests of the audience.

Medium

Not only are there numerous audiences but many different types of media which educators may select in designing a communication plan. Speeches, books, photographs, posters, letters, films, slidetapes, monographs, conversation, newspapers, television, journals, plays, telephone, even music may be used as a means to communicate a message. One educator performed folk songs to "spoof" the issue of merit pay for teachers. Positive outcomes can result from imbedding messages in art forms.

Each medium has its particular advantage. A conversation provides immediate feedback and a chance to clarify issues. Mass media such as television and newspapers can reach a large audience. Films have a unique emotional and dramatic impact. Books can be shared and re-read.

Use of multiple media for a single communication plan capitalizes on the best qualities of each medium and provides reinforcement of ideas and a variety of perspectives on an issue.[6] Combinations such as film and speech, or written material combined with a slide tape are potentially more effective than single media communication. However, the medium is probably less important overall than the strategy and message content.

Message

The message, the content of the communication, should be adapted to the level of understanding of the audience. It should be logically presented with a minimum of extraneous ideas to distract from the central message. The message should be personalized for the audience. The nature of the message may be informative, to provide an understanding of the problem. The message may consist of alternative solutions to a problem or a strong position on a particular issue. Educators should communicate to the audience that they understand the audience's stake in the issue as well as opposing interests.

Strategy

A strategy is a course of action to reach a goal. It includes the logical and psychological aspects of presenting a message. For the most part, educators will be sending messages to people who do not request them but to whom they are reaching out on their own initiative. After choosing the audience, medium and general content, educators must decide whether they wish to transmit information, persuade, or initiate dialogue.[7]

The strategy might be to use humor, threat, or immediacy. Humorous cartoons can make the same point as formal speech, creating interest and reducing anxiety. Threats, particularly to personal well-being, are also an effective means to arouse interest. Threat produces anxiety. When this is relieved by a proposed solution to problem, there is a strong possibility of acceptance of the solution. Immediacy is always an effective communication strategy. If an audience realizes, for example, that their child may receive inadequate education, the immediacy of the problem is likely to create heightened interest and action.

Persuasion is the use of logical arguments and incentives to cause another person to change his view.[8] Often, logic alone will be convincing. To be a credible persuader, it is important to be perceived as fair and truthful. Therefore, the strategy of presenting both sides of an issue is an assurance to the audience that the communicator is fully knowledgeable and is not unduly biased. If logic does not suffice, incentives for accepting a position can be offered.

A strategy of confrontation often results in inflexible positions with no resolution of opposing views. A better approach to resolving differences is to first focus on common concerns and goals and on information which is mutually acceptable. In a context of agreement, each participant in a discussion should remain attentive and should often restate what is communicated to them to avoid misunderstanding. Each should strive to remain open to new ideas and to the possibility of negotiations. Often, references to similar situations in which parties have moved closer to consensus can serve as a model for an on-going discussion and can encourage continued effort to achieve consensus.

Discussion can be initiated directly by educators in face-to-face meeting or through the use of books, radio or television broadcasts. In face-to-face interaction, educators can supply additional information and clarify ideas. In sending messages through mass media, they may lose that advantage but gain a larger audience.

The art of developing a communication plan is to select the components which will be most effective for a particular audience. The components and guidelines have been outlined here. (Examples are shown in Table 1.). Educators must use personal judgment, professional expertise, and capability to

Table 1. Examples of three communication plans.

	PLAN 1	PLAN 2	PLAN 3
Audience	Government	General Public	Government Policy-makers
Message	Information	Information (General Overview)	Information (Logical; Documentation)
Medium	Personal Communication (Telephone calls, Letters, Meetings)	Radio Television (Interview)	Personal Communication (Report; Interrogation)
Strategy	Collaboration	Immediacy; Generalization	Persuasion

use a medium to achieve the fullest benefit from their communication.

APPLICATION OF FUTURES FIELD
AND COMMUNICATION PLANNING

A current controversy concerns merit pay for teachers. Let me suggest briefly how the futures field and communication planning might assist SPOD professionals to impact the outcome of this issue.

First, SPOD professionals should become conversant in futures field literature to provide a general context to examine specific issues. They should become familiar, for example, with two major post-industrial scenarios—the service society and the self-reliant society. They should understand the nature and implications of emerging technologies, major trends in contemporary society, and the goals and issues pertinent to various interest groups.[9] This background enables educators to distinguish major trends and to place specific issues, such as merit pay, in a broad context, and to ask appropriate questions regarding this issue. Is merit pay a political strategy to ingratiate teachers or an inexpensive alternative to future raises "across the board" for the teaching profession? If so, what is the implication for the status of teachers in the future? Is merit pay part of a hidden agenda to eventually restore an educated elite? Is merit pay a palliative which will reward the best teachers without increasing the competence of less competent teachers who are the real concern?

The futures field can provide useful information, cost/benefit forecasts of outlays for merit pay over time, scenarios describing future effects of merit pay on teacher morale, occupational mobility, and parental attitudes toward teachers. Systems theory can be used to anticipate the effects of merit pay on select components of the educational system (e.g. student performance, quality of curriculum, funding) or aspects of the larger social system (e.g. taxation, talent pools, manpower planning, political strategy). The futures field provides a broad frame of reference, techniques and information to support SPOD professionals in educational decision-making and advocacy. SPOD practitioners, for example, realizing that generally the most competent teachers avail themselves of professional development, may evaluate merit pay as an inappropriate incentive for the less competent teachers. Merging the projections of futurists with their personal experience, they can design a communication plan to encourage public contemplation and enlightened decisions.

With great certainty, Alvin Toffler asserts that training and retraining will be a major thrust for education in the future.[10] Professional development for quality instruction and short-term training to gear for new technologies and careers will place SPOD in the center of educational activity. We need, however, to tend to our own professional development, to acquire skills in the futures field and communication planning so that we can finally participate in shaping the future of our profession and our society.

Let us transform the definition of education as a process to transmit the past, to prepare for the present and to create the future. Let us judge the outcome of our learning by the quality of the future we create.

REFERENCES

[1] Toffler, A. 1980 *The Third Wave*. Random House, New York.

[2] Amara, R. 1981 "Searching For Definitions and Boundries." The *Futurist*. February: pp. 25-29.

[3] Amara, R. 1981 "Searching For Definitions and Boundries." *The Futurist*. February: p. 26.

[4] Amara, R. 1981 "Which Direction Now?" *The Futurist*. June: pp. 42-46.

[5] Braid, F. R. 1981 "Communication in Organizations." *In Agricultural Research Managment*. v. 3, College, SEARCA: Laguna, Phillippines.

[6] Schramm, W. 1973 *Men, Messages and Media: A Look at Human Communication*. Harper and Row, New York.

[7] Hovland, E., Janis, L. L., Kelley, H. 1953 *Communication and Persuasion*. Yale University Press, New Haven.

[8] Kincaird, D. L., Schramm, W. 1975 *Fundamental Human Communication*. East-West Communication Institute, Honolulu, Hawaii.

[9] Marien, M. 1983 "The Two Post-Industrialisms and Higher Education." *World Future Society Bulletin*. May/June: pp. 13-26.

[10] Toffler, A. 1983 *Previews and Premises*. William Morrow and Company, New York.

Suggestions For SPOD Impact On The Future

PRACTITIONER	ADMINISTRATOR	STATE ORGANIZATION	NATIONAL ORGANIZATION
Workshop: Future Trends: Skill development for advocacy.	*Inservice:* Futures theme sessions.	*Conference:* Theme, Sessions on educational issues, future trends, analytical techniques.	same
Tabloid: Submit commentaries on Future Trends, issues, community opportunities to network.	same	*Newsletter:* Concept papers, book reviews, opinions on future of education.	same
Roster: Compile roster of experts, in-house and external, to serve as workshop presenters and staff interested in discussion groups on future-related topics.	*Roster:* Use roster for in-service; committees.	*Roster:* Consultants on futures and members from various colleges to form panels at conferences	same
Task Force: Join college and external organizations and form Future Trends Task Force.	*Task Force:* Form Future Trends Committee to report to central administration and trustees re: trends and opportunities.	*Task Force:* Same; and appoint representative to state government as advocates for organizations stance on issues. Organize policy debates for membership.	same
Curriculum: Assist teachers to include future orientation and analysis and evaluation of social issues and new technology in courses.	*Curriculum:* Develop new courses, Future Trends Program, keep Vo/Technology current.	*Curriculum:* Report on trends and curricular development in member colleges.	same

Futures Literary: Subscribe to futures field books and journals; disseminate ideas.	same Library futures Display "Future" Image For College.	same	same
Community Involvement: Become expert on an issue, candidate, technique or theory re: future development; speak and guide with future-oriented perspective.	same	same	same
Network: Collaborate on papers presentations with future-oriented colleagues outside institution.	same	same	same
Program Development: Include Future Trends topics; encourage minigrants on skills related to developing future oriented students and technical skills for faculty.	*Program Development*: Provide support for future-oriented projects and skill-building.		
Organizational Leadership: Act as change agent to introduce new ideas regarding future.	*Organizational Leadership*: Same; Act as clarifier and stimulate interest in long-range planning and innovation consistent with the trends.	*Lobby* - to state legislature regarding funding and educational policy.	*Lobby* - same to AACJC and national level.
Media: Develop videotapes to examine issues to be shown internally and externally.	*Media*: Use media at inservice and meetings to educate faculty.	*Media*: Use media at conferences.	

ABOUT THE AUTHOR

COURTNEY D. PETERSON is Vice Provost
of Mesabi Community College, Virginia,
Minnesota. Having his Ph.D. in Social,
Cultural and Educational Futures, he has
given major presentations at the First Global
Conference on the Future in Toronto and
at the International Congress on Applied
Systems Research and Cybernetics in
Acapulco. Peterson has published in four of
the top journals in the futures field and is
a member of the American Management
Association, Minnesota Futurists, the
Society for General Systems Research, and
the World Future Society. He has also made
futures presentations at the 1982 NCSPOD
Annual Conference and the NCSPOD Midwest Skills Building Conference. Formal
training as a psychologist, computer pro-
grammer and economist deepen his background.

14
Electronic Technology and the Community College: Implications for SPOD

Courtney D. Peterson

The intent of this paper is to discuss how present and future developments in electronic technology may impact community college education in general and SPOD in particular. This intent will be accomplished by including a discussion of the forces and trends in society which are contributing to an increased utilization of electronic technology, by briefly outlining the current and projected developments in electronic technology, and by presenting some implications of such developments for community colleges and SPOD.

Shane argues that human communications has gone through four revolutions.[1] The first three revolutions include the development of complex speech, writing and moveable type. The fourth revolution, which is still in its infancy and has the potential to be the most dramatic, is the electronic revolution. With the marriage of computer and telecommunications capabilities, most information utilized by humans, whether audio, video, data or graphic, can be transformed into electronic information and stored, manipulated, retrieved or transmitted to meet human and cultural needs. Given that education is a major human and cultural need and given that information and knowledge are major educational resources and/or desirable outcomes of the educational process, it is becoming increasingly clear that electronic technology is having a profound influence on the educational process.

In 1971, Clark Kerr identified educational technology as a major uncertainty facing higher education into the year 2000. The uncertainty is no longer if technology will impact higher education but how soon and how dramatic the impact will be. The Carnegie Commission on Higher Education has forecast that by the year 2000 20 percent of instruction in higher education will be electronic. Even more dramatic is their estimate that up to 80 percent of off-campus instruction may be electronic. Very few institutions of higher education have begun to explore the implications of such a dramatic shift in educational delivery methods.

MAJOR FORCES AND TRENDS

One of the primary reasons behind this oncoming shift in educational delivery methods is economic. As the cost of labor has continued to rise, the cost of electronic technology has plummeted. For example, if the cost-efficiency of Rolls Royce production had improved comparable to that of the microcomputer, its sticker price would currently be three dollars. All indications point to the continuation of this trend. Given that education is such a labor-intensive industry and given the current and projected concerns with economizing, it seems highly probably that those in control of the educational purse strings will increasingly look to more capital-intensive modes of instruction. Even though there is much emotionality concerning the alleged dehumanizing effects of electronic instruction, considerable evidence is accumulating to the contrary—that in fact electronic technology can facilitate a more humanizing, accessible and individually-oriented educational system.

A second trend contributing to the increased use of electronic technology is the information explosion. Traditional modes of information gathering, storage, retrieval and transmission simply will not be able to handle the massive amount of new information (and hopefully knowledge) being generated. It is estimated that the amount of information currently doubles every five years. This compares to a fifty-year doubling at the turn of the last century. As this rate of doubling increases, education will be forced to handle information electronically. This will allow continual updating and access to newly generated information and knowledge. The traditional forms of information dispensing, such as textbooks, lectures and journals, will in many arenas become largely nostalgic anachronisms.

A general cultural acceptance and pervasiveness of electronic technology is a third trend that will force higher education's hand in utilizing electronic delivery. With our society becoming electronically networked, with the dramatic increase in the number of home computers, with the expansion of cable, fiber optics and direct satellite broadcasting (DSB), and with the rapid growth in information data bases and data base networking, individuals, in the comfort of their homes or places of work, will be able to access the types of educational opportunities now largely monopolized by higher education. Those institutions that refuse to participate in such access will simply be bypassed.

The final trend contributing to the utilization of electronic technology is technological development itself, both computer and telecommunications technology. Fuller's concept of ephemeralization—doing more with less—comes to mind in describing hardware advances. In computer technology this includes increased miniaturization, capacity and speed, with comparable decreases in costs. The costs of logic devices and computer memory have been decreasing by 25 and 40 percent per year respectively. The amount of circuitry per area doubles every two years. (Current technology allows the entire contents of the Encyclopedia Britannica to fit on an area the size of a postage stamp.) And the costs of energy consumption and the size of computers of comparable power have decreased by a factor of 10,000 since the 1950s.

Projected developments appear to be as dramatic. It has been forecast that by 1989 IBM will have developed a six-inch cube computer equal in capacity to current IBM computer power at seven times current operating speed. Moving into the 21st century, we can look forward to biochips—

grown microprocessors capable of direct brain/computer interfacing with millions of times more memory capacity than presently available.

Advances in telecommunications technology are as impressive and portend a networked, real-time society. The telephone has networked our society, but its information carrying capacity is limited. New technologies dramatically increase information carrying capacity and often allow for portability. These technologies include expansion of the cable system, microwave transmission, low-power VHF and UHF stations, satellite laser transmission, direct satellite broadcast, videotext and fiber optics.

Satellites are already a part of our information world; however, their numbers and information-carrying capacity are minuscule compared to what will develop. As satellites move from microwave transmission to laser transmission, channel capacity will increase from hundreds to millions. Theoretically, one laser beam can transmit eighty million color TV channels.

As satellites become larger and more powerful, earth receivers will become smaller and more complex. This is what is known as complexity inversion and allows for direct satellite broadcast into homes. Presently, two-foot diameter satellite dish receivers are available. By the year 2000, portable three-inch telephone receivers and portable six-inch receivers with audio and data processing (computer) capability will be functional.

Developments in fiber optics are as impressive. The information-carrying capacity of a single glass fiber, one fifth the thicknesss of a human hair, is phenomenal. Currently, one pair of glass fibers (allowing for two-way communication) can carry 4,000 conversations. Projected developments in fiber optics technology will up this capacity considerably. In comparison, the carrying capacity of a pair of regular telephone wires is about twenty-four conversations.

As homes, businesses and schools become networked with fiber optics, direct satellite broadcast and portable receiving, computing and transmitting technology, each individual will have access to an informational cornucopia. Imagine the majority of homes and individuals with access to virtually un unlimited amount of information. Imagine each home networked with an information utility, much like the current gas, electric and water service available to most Americans. Imagine computer systems with the ability to sense, perceive, reason, create, make decisions and think— systems that are so complex that it may be impossible to distinguish their reasoning and problem-solving processes from that of humans. These are the systems that encompass artificial intelligence, with specific problem-solving and reasoning processes programmed as so-called "expert systems."

"Expert systems" are specialized computer programs with state-of-the-art information and knowledge about a particular topic, combined with reasoning and heuristic problem-solving capability. Examples of existing systems are PUFF and MACSYMA. PUFF is used to diagnose lung problems and has a 85 percent concordance with human diagnosis. MACSYMA is a program that solves general math problems, algebraic equations, and differential and integral calculus. Joseph argues that no better mathematical system exists—either machine or human. Additionally he argues that "current expert systems show that when compared with traditional sources of knowledge (books, tapes, classrooms) present and future knowledge based expert systems are (and will be) 10 to 1,000 times more complete, precise, current and comprehensible."[2]

Given these realities and reasonable forecasts, the limitations of time and space for accessing information and knowledge will virtually be eliminated. Individuals will have access to cultural events, educational programs and courses, research sources, business information, current events and news, advertising, computer and human experts, and on and on. In such a rich informational environment, the traditional educational establishment will no longer have a monopoly as repository and distributor of information and knowledge, nor on academic credentialing. For example, if an individual wants to acquire a basic knowledge of psychology, he will have access to any number of psychology data bases, whether human, machine or any combination. This diversity will hold true for most disciplines and areas of knowledge. Other scenarios are available, but one of the most powerfully convincing is that of a society increasingly decentralized by the power of electronic knowledge and informational systems.

COMMUNITY COLLEGES AND SPOD

The possible implications of electronic technology for community colleges and SPOD are potentially so numerous and dramatic that only a few can be mentioned in this paper. Electronic technology will continue the trends in postsecondary education of decentralization, democratization, access and life-long learning. Because community colleges have been at the vanguard of these trends, if they position themselves properly, they will be able to benefit most from electronic technology.

In this environment, the College Without Walls concept will rapidly expand. Colleges will often be defined in terms of educational/communication networks and linkages rather than in terms of buildings or locations. Faculty and curricula will no longer be identified exclusively with particular institutions; instead, students and citizens will have delayed and/or real-time 24-hour access to electronically delivered lectures, books, journals, courses, programs, seminars, interest groups, demonstrations and professors originating from a region, a state, a nation or the world. This type of participation will permit full audio, video and data contact, with minimal regard for space, time and location limitations.

The potential reality of such an educational environment requires that if community colleges are to benefit from electronic technology, a critical rethinking of institutional roles, organizational structures, course delivery systems, staff roles and functions, and the nature and characteristics of students served will be required. What better role for SPODers than to be intimately involved in such a rethinking? How better to practice staff, program and organizational development than vis-a-vis electronic technology?

Staff development will become a priority issue as electronic technology exerts its influence on postsecondary education. Community colleges will not be immune from the training/retraining impacts of electronic technology; consequently, *all* faculty and staff will need competencies in computers and electronic curriculum delivery. The characteristics and major roles of the faculty and staff will also change. The number of part-time and adjunct instructors will most likely increase, as will the number and importance of electronics and media specialists. The role of the traditional faculty member will shift from that of lecturer and purveyor of knowledge and information to that of seminar leader, course manager, academic counselor, and courseware and software designer.

As more and more instruction is done electronically, it may be argued that individual student/faculty contact will actually increase. Many futurists argue that in addition to training in electronic technology and in their specific discipline(s), future faculty members will need considerably more training in academic advising, counseling and vocational/career guidance. What better challenge for staff developers than to help facilitate the movement of their institution and its faculty into the Information Age?

Innovations in program development will involve both the networking and coordination of programs delivered via electronic technology and the development of curricula for new programs. Many programs will not be available from a single institution, but from consortia and cooperative networks spread over large geographical areas. Considerable planning and coordination will be required to facilitate such instructional systems. Even programs offered by a single institution or within a limited geographical region will require much research and innovation. In addition to shaping curricula to meet the demands and opportunities of electronic delivery, foresight will be needed in selecting and designing programs that meet the needs of both the economy and the students served. Given the retraining needs of the Information Age, the era of the relatively permanent transfer and occupational curriculum will be an anachronism for most institutions. Instead, program developers must become educational/career futurists, continually projecting institutional program needs three to five years into the future.

The final namesake of the SPODer—and the most all encompassing—is that of organizational developer. The impacts of electronic technology on educational institutions will require the services of individuals trained in the redesigning and restructuring of Information Age organizations. Obviously staff and program development are part of this process of organizational change.

These organizations/networks/consortia/cooperatives will be characterized by complexity and transience, with lines of authority and organizational boundaries constantly being redefined and reshaped. Colleges and universities will enter into a myriad of networking agreements necessary to provide their services. Such agreements will include organizations that are profit and nonprofit, public and nonpublic, religious and nonreligious, etc. For example, a community college may network with a university, a business and a nonprofit organization to provide a one-time program offering.

Such an arrangment exemplifies Toffler's concept of adhocracy: a temporary organizational structure created to solve a one-time problem or serve a one-time need. Once the problem is solved or the need fulfilled the structure is disbanded. Ad-hocracies will increasingly characterize organizational structures in the Information Age.

Much of this organizational flexibility and networking already exists among the more creative community colleges. However, electronic technology will accelerate this process and be the primary force behind the need for perpetual staff, program and organizational development.

CONCLUSION

Given the present and future world of electronic technology and change, the SPODer must simultaneously be a generalist and a specialist—an individual who can conceptualize and work from a systemic, organizational perspective, yet understand and work with the details of a staff development project or program curriculum design.

A geniune SPODer must be a futurist, with an ability to function in a world of constant flux and change. The challenges and opportunities for SPODers working in such a period of transition are limitless. From an institutional perspective, the major task will be the necessity of reconceptualizing purpose, mission and goals. From a personal, very human perspective, the most formidable challenge will be to help people find meaningful work in the Information Age.

SPODers must embrace these challenges and the accompanying uncertainty surrounding them, for only by accepting uncertainty as a constant companion will individuals and institutions remain adaptable enough to survive the rites of passage into the 21st century.

REFERENCES

[1]Shane, H. 1982 "The Silicon Age and Education." *Phi Delta Kappan.* January:303-308.

[2]Joseph, E. 1982 "What's Ahead For Intelligence Amplification." *Futurics.* 6(2):35-38.

RECOMMENDATIONS FOR:

SPOD Practitioners

1. Read broadly and extensively in Futures and science journals.
2. Develop and coordinate staff development workshops on electronic/instructional technology.
3. Keep faculty and staff abreast of the latest and future developments in electronic/instructional technology by distributing appropriate literature.
4. Encourage faculty attendance at conferences addressing the issue of electronic/instructional technology.

Local Colleges

1. Establish a standing committee on electronic/instructional technology.
2. Implement staff development workshops on electronic/instructional technology.
3. Work to develop intercollegiate electronic/instructional technology consortia.

State Associations

1. Establish a standing committee on electronic/instructional technology.
2. Develop and coordinate workshops on electronic/instructional technology.
3. Feature electronic/instructional technology news, trends, developments, etc. in state newsletters.

NCSPOD Executive Board

1. Feature electronic/instructional technology news, trends, developments, etc. in the national newsletter.
2. Provide for an electronic/instructional technology track or electronic/instructional technology sessions at the National Conference.
3. Develop and coordinate workshops on electronic/instructional technology at the National Conference and/or regional conferences.

SUGGESTED READINGS

Cornish, Edward, ed. *Communications Tomorrow*, Washington, D.C.: World Future Society, 1982.

A collection of articles on communications that first appeared in *The Futurist*. An excellent single source on the latest in electronic technology and speculation on its impact on society.

Didsbury, Howard F. Jr., ed. *Communications and the Future: Prospects, Promises, and Problems*, Washington, D.C.: World Future Society, 1982.

A collection of 46 papers on communications and electronic technology presented at the World Future Society Fourth General Assembly, July, 1983.

Evans, Christopher, *The Micro Millennium*. New York: Washington Square Press, 1979.

An excellent history of computer technology and forecasts of future developments.

Informational Technology & Its Impact on American Education, Office of Technology Assessment, November, 1982.

This book is available from the Superintendent of Documents, U.S. Government Printing Office, Washington, D.C. 20402

Marien, Michael. "Touring Futures: An Incomplete Guide to the Literature," *The Futurist*, 17(2): 12-21, April, 1983.

An excellent review of the most popular personalities in the Futures field and a summary of critical bibliography.

The Futurist: A monthly publication of the World Future Society. An excellent journal covering the general concerns of the Futures field.

ABOUT THE AUTHOR

ROLAND TERRELL is Associate Vice President for College Relations and Development at Florida Junior College at Jacksonville, Florida, and has a doctorate. He is founding President of NCSPOD and founding President of the Florida Council for Staff, Program and Organizational Development.

15
Institutionalization:
A Step Into the Future

Roland Terrell

After three years of recession, leaders in staff, program and organization development are still asking, "Is staff, program, and organization development dead in community colleges?"

The effects felt from the budget cuts experienced by community colleges across the country are still being reported. Programs have been eliminated, program coordinators and directors have been removed or transferred, and there has been a drastic curtailment in development activities. Florida, a national leader for over fifteen years, was not spared the effects of the budget-cutting storm. Legislative cuts forced community college presidents to ask for a moratorium for one year in order to gain some needed assistance in meeting local needs.

Now that the storm is subsiding, and we find ourselves reflecting on what happened and why, let us use this as an opportunity to rebuild our programs on a more secure basis this time. If there is to be security, then we must determine how we can become more of a part of the institution in which we serve. We must institutionalize our programs.

Yet, there is already evidence that we will repeat our

mistakes from the past.

Since the 1970s, the staff, program and organization development movement has focused on a variety of goals, all of which were necessary. The movement was concerned almost solely with the development of a financial foundation for funding development activities on a consistent basis.

The formula used in Florida became a national solution to be applied elsewhere. Practitioners sought security in achieving positive commitment from their institutional leaders. Presidents were asked constantly to make public statements of support for development activities. Then, like adolescents in search of themselves, we have looked introspectively to determine our roles, competencies and organizational features. Our conferences and workshops have directed attention to the role for the development director, the special relationships to the president, potential funding sources, competency models for the practitioner, and the latest fad for being popular with the faculty and administration that focused on the use of time, the stresses that we encounter, or how to motivate others to do more and more with less and less.

For all of our characteristic foresight, as planners or practitioners, we have failed to understand that these activities and topics are input-oriented and do not represent outcomes that have any long-range value to institutions. Like all practice-oriented thinkers, we have placed a high value on the need to have a higher frequency and number of activities that are not consciously related to program outcomes or a theoretical approach to resolving institutional needs. There has been constant use of the trial and error approach, hoping to hit the mark and bring popular success.

There is clearly a need to establish a new direction in our thinking about the mission for SPOD in community colleges. In order to do this, we must look at the organizational structure in our institutions and learn how it functions. There must be a greater understanding about what is meant by institutional outcomes and how they are met by all functions within the college. It is through the concepts related to institutionalization that I suggest that we must align our SPOD programs and begin to rebuild.

THE CONCEPT OF INSTITUTIONALIZATION

Institutionalization is an organizational characteristic that describes when a function of the organization has been accepted as having value in meeting institutional outcomes. In organization theory, there is the principle of functions as a means of describing the structure within an institution. The functions are described as processes that provide support to those activities that are required to achieve the stated outcomes of the organization. Functions in a community college include: Personnel, Finance, Curriculum and Instruction, Facilities, Equal Access and Equal Opportunity, Accounting, Purchasing, Foundation, Resource Development, Alumni Relations, Information Services, Public Relations, Data Processing, Student Services, Financial Aid and Athletics. Staff, program and organization development in most institutions has not been identified as a function that is valued to the extent that it is included in the organizational chart of important functions. When a function is listed, then institutionalization is said to have occurred.

BENEFITS OF INSTITUTIONALIZATION

1. SPOD as a function will have a stated role and purpose that brings a level of acceptance within the institution. This is a desirable status to attain. It will cause the emergence of support from all areas and levels within the college.

2. Financial support will follow those objectives which are included in the group of functions that are valued. Such support will increase as the perceived value of the function increases.

3. Commitment as a level of the intensity of support will be evident by the existence of specially tilted institutional leaders in an institutionalized function.

4. A level of security is realized for institutionalized functions. There is less of a tendency to abolish those functions that have such a level of support.

5. Institutionalized functions play more of a role in meeting the institution's stated outcomes and are greatly valued as such.

INSTITUTIONALIZING SPOD AS A FUNCTION

There are a number of considerations to be made by local staff, program and organization development leaders in community colleges.

1. Review the organization development literature that best describes the structure that is found in your institution in order to develop a greater knowledge of how organizations are structured. Attending workshops and seminars that focus on management development and organization development is also helpful.

2. Review the organization chart for your college. Most organization charts reflect the positions that are to be found in the college. If there is no organization chart that provides the functions, then you should attempt to develop one.

3. Given an outline of the college's functions, develop an analysis of what activities, events, tasks, and objectives are most commonly identified with each functional area. It is extremely critical that a detailed analysis be conducted and that a high level of comprehension be achieved.

4. Determine from the functional analysis what activities, objectives, tasks, and events are most related to staff, program and organization development interests. Personnel, curriculum and instruction, and planning are usually identified. Training as an activity in the personnel function is a consideration.

5. Assess if this activity can best be served from being a part of the personnel function or may be better preformed in another location in the organization. Present a clear argument with a plan for accomplishing this activity in another functional area, which may be called staff development.

6. Staff, program and organization development are each separate functions and should be included in your analysis. A comparison of your functional analysis in these areas should be made with possible target functions.

7. Determine the best strategic positioning for those activities with which you are most aligned. You may be more successful to start a staff development activity as a part of the personnel function. To the contrary, you may be more successful to include it as a part of the instruction function. Only if the activity is sufficient in scope and already has a

high level of commitment will you be successful in establishing the activity as a separate function.

8. Analyze the sources of power in the institution. The traditional sources are the president, executive vice-presidents, provosts and deans. Develop both professional and personal relationships. Be seen as positive and resourceful. Develop a good track record for achieving results.

9. Provide services that are timely, needed and successful with employee groups throughout the college. Faculty have considerable influence and their evaluation of the benefits provided by your functional area is valuable.

10. Market your functional area. Determine the needs of the college and develop services, tasks, activities, and events that will help your target groups be successful. Be worthy of being listed as a function. Gain recognition at the local, state and national levels for your function. Select outstanding personnel and be supportive in their professional accomplishments. Develop a positive image of your area that includes a high degree of competency for all personnel, assures accuracy and quality in performance, and the ability to get the job done.

A STRATEGIC PLAN FOR INSTITUTIONALIZATION

There is an advantage to organizing our efforts to institutionalize. There will be a greater likelihood for success if we do so. This effort will have to include local practitioners, state associations and the National Council for SPOD.

Local Practitioners:

1. Challenge what you are now doing as the best way to be of assistance to your institution. It has been said before, "There must be a better way to do this." If you have been saying similar things to yourself and now others, start looking at another plan.

2. Look to those institutions that have an organizational plan that includes a philosophy, mission and institutional goals and objectives, a functional analysis of the organization, administrative procedures that are current and detailed, and competency based job descriptions.

3. Learn more about those institutions which have established SPOD programs that have been around in the ten- to fifteen-year range. They *must* be institutionalized. No one exists that long unless that is the case.

4. Be more political. This does not mean to be more aggressive or assertive. Determine the sources of power, develop coalitions and be ready to ask for support in return for your support.

5. Develop a theoretical sense of what an organization is and how it functions. Don't be so caught up in the "doing of things" and action oriented all of the time. Stop, step back and begin to reflect about the nature of things, criteria, and policies. Then develop strategies that will put your theory into operation.

State Associations:

1. Develop a new objective for the association that promotes the institutionalization of all staff, program and organization development offices.

2. Develop a list of colleges and activities that have institutionalized in their state. Circulate such lists and call attention to those institutions in their literature, conferences, and other activities.

3. Develop workshops that teach other practitioners how these identified institutionalized activities can work in their college.

4. Develop a new function for associations that provides service consultants and task forces that are available on site for colleges. This service function would address only the functional activities that should be institutionalized in colleges in their state.

5. Re-examine the mission and objectives for the state association through a state conference that addresses the needs of its individual and college members. A theoretical basis for action is now needed.

National Council for SPOD:

1. Develop a national objective that promotes the institutionalization of SPOD in member colleges.

2. Develop a national list of colleges that have been institutionalized or have features of their programs that have been.

3. Develop a list of individuals and groups that may offer their services to member colleges in an effort to provide assistance to institutionalize.

4. Provide grants to university doctoral students who wish to conduct research in the concept of institutionalization in SPOD activities in community colleges.

5. Develop a new publication that is a case study of how an institution has institutionalized an activity, event, task, or service.

6. Develop a national conference on "Institutionalizing SPOD in the Community Colleges."

7. Provide more support, both financial and professional, to the development of theories related to staff, program and organization development. Support publications, conferences and workshops, research studies and individual efforts that develop new ways of thinking about how SPOD functions can best be a part of community colleges.

THE FUTURE FOR THE STAFF, PROGRAM AND ORGANIZATION DEVELOPMENT MOVEMENT

A favorite story of mine concerns the time that Charlie Brown, the comic strip character, was told by his teacher that he was a great disappointment to her and that she was sending him to the principal's office because he had not lived up to his great potential. The principal told Charlie Brown that he was sending him home because he also felt that Charlie was not living up to his great potential. On the way home, Lucy, lying in wait, jumped from behind a bush, and bopped Charlie in the nose, and told him that he was a disappointment to her because everyone said that he was not living up to his great potential. As he arrived home, his mother stepped to the door and scolded him, saying, "Charlie Brown, you are a great disappointment to your father and me, because you are not living up to your great potential." In the last frame of the comic strip, we see Charlie sitting on the curb with his big moon shaped head in his hands saying, "You know. . . there is no greater burden than a great potential."

There is no greater burden than a great potential that is not achieved. The staff, program and organization development movement must continue to prove itself every day. We have taken on a great responsibility to represent the needs, the issues and the problems to be found in our field.

The future is literally in our hands and we must ask ourselves if we are doing enough about it. This is a time for renewal and setting new challenges. Unless we find ways to institutionalize more SPOD programs our record for accomplishments will mean less to those who are watching to see if we accomplish our great potential.

SUGGESTED RESOURCES

Terrell, R. 1983 "The Institutionalization of SPOD." *The Journal of Staff, Program and Organization Development,* 1:7-10.

Wright, F. 1983 "Weaving SPOD Into the Fabric of the College: Integrating People, Program and Finances," unpublished paper, NCSPOD National Congress, Kansas City, Kansas.

INDEX

Futures network:
  how to organize, 55-58
  key ingredients to formation, 58
Futurists:
  criticisms of education, 44-48,
  educational critique, 42-46
  educators as, 125-136
  prescriptions for education, 46-
    48
  rationale, 39-42
  recommendations for colleges,
    146
  recommendations for SPOD
    practitioners, 146
  scientific-technological, 41-42
  social, 42
  suggested readings, 147
  visionary-alternatives, 42-43

G

Garrison, Don C., 78
Geier, John G., 24
Glines, Donald, 46-47

H

Haring, Ed, 4, 54
Hawaii:
  community colleges, 104-113
  future of SPOD in, 112-113
  history and organization of
    system, 106
  staff development, 106-108
Hubbard, Barbara Max, 15
Human resource development:
  and instruction, 102
  and technology, 99-100
  investments in, 90
  policy for U.S., 80, 90
Humanities, role in education, 39

I

Information:
  age, 143-144
  explosion, 138-139
In Search of Excellence (Peters
  and Waterman), 23, 62-64, 66,
  105, 121

Institutionalization of SPOD:
  a strategic plan, 153-155
  benefits of, 151
  concept of, 3, 151
  guide for NCSPOD, 154-155
  guide for practitioners, 153-154
  guide for state associations, 154
  steps in, 152-153

J

Job Training Partnership Act, 73,
  82
Joseph, Earl, 141

K

Kahn, Herman, 42, 43
Keller, George, 28
Kellogg Foundation, 80
Kerr, Clark, 138
Kierstead, Frederick, 46, 47
Kindler, Herbert S., 19, 20, 22
Krishnamurti, Jiddu, 37-38

L

League for Innovation, 23
Learning:
  future-oriented system, 48-50
  life-long, 46, 85
Learning for Tomorrow (Toffler),
  46

Mc

McCabe, Robert, 23

M

Meeting Learners' Needs Through
  Telecommunications (Edger-
  ton), 120
Megatrends (Naisbitt), 7, 56, 57,
  79
MXC Learning System, 47

T

Technical education, 39
Technology:
  advances, 70, 72-73
  and personal growth, 99
  and the community/technical
    college, 137-145
  artificial intelligence, 141
  consequences of, 79-85
  development of, 139-140
  economic implications of, 138
  educational, 42, 63, 115-121
  electronic, 137-145
  implications for staff develop-
    ment, 120-121, 137-145
  pervasiveness of, 139
  trends, 138-142
Telecommunications:
  administration, 119
  advances in, 140
  computer literacy in, 117
  faculty training, 119-120
  fiber optics in, 140-141
  in the home, 140-141
  overview of a system, 117-120
  programming, 118-119
  satellites, 140
Terrell, Roland, 4, 148
Theobald, Robert, 15
The Third Wave (Toffler), 116

*To Strengthen Quality in Higher
  Education* (The National Com-
  mission on Higher Education
  Issues), 72
Toffler, Alvin, 42, 46, 116, 144
Truman Commission Report, 21
Tsunoda, Joyce S., 104
The Turning Point (Capra), 7

U

Unionism in education, 61-62

V

Veregge, Marvin, 104

W

Waterman, Robert Jr., 23, 24, 32,
  62, 105, 121
Willett, Lynn H., 12, 54
Wilson Campus School, 47
Wolin, Sheldon, 38-39
Work:
  automation in, 82
  retraining programs, 82
  role of community college as
    related to, 79-85
World Future Society, 6, 13, 36,
  136
World-view of western society, 40